CONNECTED RISK

Conquering the Perilous Risk Exposure Gap

RICHARD F. CHAMBERS

SPONSORED BY

Published by Fina Press, an imprint of WoW Media Publishing Consultants, LLC
33 Ocean Palm Villa North
Flagler Beach, FL 32136

Sponsored by:

AuditBoard transforms how audit, risk, ESG, and InfoSec professionals manage today's dynamic risk landscape with a modern, connected platform that engages the front lines, surfaces the risks that matter, and drives better strategic decision-making.

Print ISBN-13: 978-1-963998-07-8
ePUB ISBN: 978-1-963998-06-1
LCCN: 2024912644

30 29 28 27 26 25 24 LSI 1 2 3 4 5 6 7 8 9

Contents

Part 5 – Futureproofing for Risk Resilience

List of Illustrations

List of Acronyms

AAA = American Accounting Association
AI = Artificial intelligence
AICPA = American Institute of Certified Public Accountants
AMA = American Management Association
AMD = Advanced Micro Devices
CAE = Chief audit executive
CSRD = European Union's Corporate Sustainability Reporting Directive
COSO = The Committee of Sponsoring Organizations of the Treadway Commission
ECIIA = European Confederation of Institutes of Internal Auditing
ERM = Enterprise risk management
ESG = Environmental, social, governance
ESRS = European Sustainability Reporting Standards
EY = Ernst & Young
FEI = Financial Executives International
FERMA = Federation of European Risk Management Associations
GRC = Governance, risk, and compliance
IAF = Internal Audit Foundation
IIA = The Institute of Internal Auditors
IFRS = International Financial Reporting Standards
IMA = Institute of Management Accountants
IPPF = International professional practices framework
IRM = Integrated risk management
ISO = The International Organization for Standardization
ISSB = International Sustainability Standards Board

KRI = Key risk indicator

PwC = PricewaterhouseCoopers

RV^2 = the "compounding impact of risk velocity and volatility"

SEC = Securities and Exchange Commission

SoD = Segregation of duties

SOX = Sarbanes-Oxley Act

USPS = United States Postal Service

WEF = World Economic Forum

Foreword

I have had the privilege of knowing Richard for many years both professionally and as a friend. He has supported my career and more recently been a vital friend in my role as CEO of SWAP Internal Audit Services, serving on our board of directors. In all Richard does, he continues to inspire and elevate our profession.

I recall an individual saying to me, "Why did you ask Richard to join your board? He is internal audit and may make you look inadequate."

My response was, "That is exactly why. I want the best in the business on the SWAP board, and Richard will not make me feel inadequate—I will just continue to learn." For three years, I have done precisely that. His insights, knowledge, wisdom, and the generosity of his time have been a huge inspiration to me, which continues to this day. So, when Richard asked me if I would write the foreword to his new book, *Connected Risk: Conquering the Perilous Risk Exposure Gap*, it was not only an honor, but the answer was an immediate "Yes, please!"

In this book, Richard relates how the "risk landscape is forever changed, as one disruptive risk event after another asserts its profound interconnectedness and inability to be contained." The relevance of this statement is not lost on me when I consider the many notable corporate failings of recent decades.

One vivid example of the catastrophic results common when interconnected risks are not adequately found, managed, or mitigated was the 2008 collapse of global financial services firm Lehman Brothers. The firm significantly invested in subprime mortgage-backed securities, such that any deterioration would have far-reaching effects across multiple financial instruments. Despite knowing this, the portfolio was insufficiently diverse and could not absorb any shock from a subprime market downturn. Lehman

Brothers also used excessive leverage (a ratio of more than 40:1), and yet did not keep sufficient capital reserves as a buffer against potential losses.

The failure to identify these interconnected risks resulted in widespread failings and loss of confidence in the financial markets. Consumers certainly felt those effects with increases in mortgage rates; I personally suffered with negative equity.

This experience—of a corporate failure creating a chain reaction impacting an entire industry and, ultimately, the average consumer—has become all too familiar. From Equifax and Facebook's data breaches to Boeing's quality breakdowns to far-reaching frauds at companies like FTX, Theranos, and Wirecard, risks' ripple effects are increasingly apparent.

So, Richard's latest offering is both relevant and timely. He skillfully sets the scene in the era of permacrisis and establishes the stakes: the widening risk exposure gap. As well as his own views, he draws on a wide array of surveys, reports, and analyses. Because Richard is focused on inspiring action, he outlines key attributes of connected risk thinkers, and offering practical solutions for influencing change, aligning terms and technologies, and futureproofing for risk resilience. Point by point, Richard makes the case for "connected risk," a reinvigorated approach to risk management that empowers professionals to improve how they work together across all three lines.

I often speak to people about risk—in fact, I occasionally deliver training on enterprise risk management (ERM). But I am often left with a sense of disillusionment. It is clear to me that many, if not most, see ERM as a process. Whilst it is a framework designed to minimize loss and maximize opportunities by taking a holistic approach, often the interplay between different risks is not fully understood due to their complexity and interconnectedness. It is also clear that many organizations undertake risk assessments only periodically, so there is no continuous monitoring of key risk indicators (KRIs)—which, as Richard says, leaves companies vulnerable. Achieving resilience in today's risk conditions mandates that companies do more.

At SWAP, we have worked hard with all three lines in multiple organizations to ensure that we have a continuous risk assessment, providing real-time visibility into risk via a dynamic dashboard that is available 24/7. Rethinking traditional ways of working, embracing the right technology solutions as capacity multipliers, and focusing on the right risks and their key interconnections should truly result in fewer corporate failings.

In Richard's previous book, *Agents of Change: Internal Auditors in the Era of Permacrisis (Second Edition)*, he provides an apt description from author David Shariatmadari to describe permacrisis: "a term that perfectly embodies the dizzying sense of lurching from one unprecedented event to another, as we wonder bleakly what new horrors might be around the corner."

As audit, risk, compliance, and information security professionals, we must learn to thrive and embrace a world driven by ambiguity, complexity, and even the incomprehensible. In fact, Richard suggests we go further, becoming "connected risk change agents," giving a name to the people critically needed to catalyze risk management transformation.

In all of Richard's books, I love his shared experience throughout his career, painting real-life stories that bring theory into color. But his unique ability to put down on paper what many are thinking—and yet unprepared to say—is what makes him such an important voice.

This latest book from Richard, like his earlier offerings, should be considered an addition to every internal auditor's toolkit. However, I would go further, as this book is also highly relevant to risk-focused professionals across all three lines. As AuditBoard President and CEO, Scott Arnold, recently said, Richard's books are a "must-read" for anyone looking to elevate their impact and profession.

Thank you, Richard. I hope there are more books in the pipeline, so that your knowledge and wisdom continue to drive risk management forward.

—David Hill
CEO, SWAP Internal Audit Services

Acknowledgments

In each of the previous books I have written, I have acknowledged that authorship was a rewarding experience in my own professional journey. Each time, I did so with little appreciation for the learning experiences that lay ahead—and that would make the next book inevitable. As with all of my professional endeavors, this book would not have been possible without the encouragement and support of so many family members, friends, and colleagues. My wife, Kim, continues to be an extraordinary source of support and encouragement. Her words of advice, reassurance, patience, and understanding over the past 35 years have been instrumental to any success I have had in a professional journey that now spans nearly half a century. My parents, Linville and Mildred Chambers, were a huge inspiration and taught me at an early age the importance of treating those around me with love and respect. My talented and beautiful daughters, Natalie McElwee, Christina Morton, and Allison Chambers, and their families are more important than any professional legacies I could ever leave.

Thanks to AuditBoard for having confidence in me and for sponsoring my full published catalog of what is now four books. I will be eternally indebted to Heather Reagan for all of her help in organizing and writing this book. She understood my vision for this project and brought boundless energy and an extraordinary writing style to the project. Thanks to Erin Sweeney for her instrumental role in bringing this book to life. Her organization, communication, and writing skills are second to none. Thanks also to my longtime friend Paul Sobel for generously sharing his time and insights, and to Tom O'Reilly for his technical advice on connected risk and patiently working with the writing team throughout the project. Thanks to John Reese for his inspiration for the book and unwavering support, and to Scott Arnold for his continued partnership, vision, and advocacy. Thanks to all those who advised us on the project, including Devin Davis, Scott Garner, Matt Nelson, Lizzie Cantor, Anton Dam, Rajiv Makhijani, Mary Krzoska, and Sydney Price.

Thanks to Lillian McAnally and WoW Media Publishing for their award-winning expertise in bringing this book to readers around the world. Lillian has been my publishing partner since my first book appeared on bookshelves in 2014, and today I am proud to call WoW Media the publisher of my entire catalog.

Finally, I would be remiss if I didn't once again thank the countless men and women I have had the privilege of calling colleagues over the course of my soon-to-be 50-year career. They have inspired and challenged me to strive for excellence. I learned much from them about professionalism, growth, resilience, and the power of collaboration.

Introduction

When I published my third book in 2021, I assumed my body of manuscripts was complete. After all, a trilogy has a nice ring to it.

My first book, *Lessons Learned on the Audit Trail*, is a semi-autobiographical look at my experiences in internal auditing over nearly 40 years (at that time). My intent was to impart a bit of wisdom based on my exposure to hundreds, if not thousands, of internal auditors and audits that shaped my views of risk, independent assurance, good governance, and the value internal audit provides. Five years after its initial publication, I updated the book to reflect new lessons learned as a result of heightened risk velocity and volatility. The updated version was titled *The Speed of Risk: Lessons Learned on the Audit Trail, 2nd Edition*, and it proved equally popular with readers.

Three years after the first edition of *Lessons Learned on the Audit Trail*, I released my second book, *Trusted Advisors: Key Attributes of Outstanding Internal Auditors*. My research for the book included conducting surveys and interviews with a diverse group of leading internal auditors. Through these conversations, I discovered key traits that define exceptional internal auditors—those who have secured a place at the table and are recognized as trusted advisors within their organizations. The book explores attributes such as ethical resilience, critical thinking, business acumen, intellectual curiosity, dynamic communication skills, and effective relationship building.

The final installment in the intended trilogy was *Agents of Change: Internal Audit in an Era of Disruption*. I wrote the book as a call to action for internal audit practitioners at all levels. It reviews the evolution and current state of the profession and provides a road map for the revolution—not just evolution—that must come for internal auditing. Only three years later, I would update

Agents of Change to account for the extraordinary disruption the world has experienced in the first half of the 2020s.

As I updated new editions of all three books for a new publisher in early 2024, I was struck by the realization that the last word on risk management cannot be written in an era of perpetual risk-induced disruption. If we have learned anything in the first half of the 2020s, it is that the traditional "three lines" approach creates its own set of risks. Management cannot simply assess risks and design and implement controls in isolation from those who monitor or provide assurance on risks. Those who monitor risks cannot do so in silos that enable no engagement with risk owners or those who ultimately provide assurance on its effectiveness. Further, internal auditors cannot sit contently in the third line awaiting their turn to identify the other lines' shortcomings.

In today's world, these silos must give way to collaboration fueled by technology and a common objective—the success of the enterprise served by each player in the three lines. We must collaborate, coordinate, and communicate with each other to not only protect, but create organizational value. The approach I advocate in this book is one I refer to as "connected risk"—a modern, cross-functional, technology-enabled approach to managing risk across the enterprise that empowers new ways of collaborating across traditional lines.

I've been advocating a connected approach for years, most often through the lens of internal audit. I have always felt that internal auditors can and should be catalysts for positive change in their organizations. After I left my position as CEO of The Institute of Internal Auditors (IIA) in early 2021, I sought to join forces with a strategic partner that would support me in continuing to champion internal auditing. I chose AuditBoard in large part because I immediately saw how our missions and ways of thinking aligned. Our journey since then has been a truly remarkable, rewarding collaboration that has meaningfully expanded both my mission and message. My work with AuditBoard has allowed me a broader view of the current state of risk management, and an expanded platform to continue advocating for positive change. I am continually inspired by the work we are doing together.

This context brings me back to connected risk, which I consider the kryptonite to siloed risk management. Connected risk helps organizations reduce silos, more effectively leverage technology, and improve how teams work together to protect and create value for their organizations. It requires the involvement of all of the key risk players, as well as buy-in and support from the board, audit committee, and C-suite. Connected risk brings together all these players' perspectives, capabilities, and strengths to drive more benefit from the valuable risk resources organizations already have.

My objective in this book is to advance the new way of thinking required for effective risk management in the era of permacrisis and beyond. I am reaching beyond my usual audience to appeal to key risk players across all three lines, including not only internal auditors, but also professionals in risk management, information security (InfoSec), compliance, the C-suite, and other members of front-line management. Drawing on my perspective as an internal auditor, business leader, and board member, I lay out the case for connected risk in five parts.

Part 1 begins by examining the conditions we're working under—the era of permacrisis. We survey the evidence, inspecting the root causes behind the speed of risk and the devastating value destruction effects we have observed as a result. We also explore how some organizations have used effective risk management for value creation, embracing risks as strategic opportunities.

Part 2 assesses the phenomenon of the "risk exposure gap": what it is, how it has emerged, and the existential threats it presents for many organizations.

Part 3 considers how the conditions, causes, and effects of the risk exposure gap are impacting risk management and organizations, and starts laying out potential solutions. In particular, I introduce a companion to the classic Three Lines Model that I call the Connected Risk Model.

Part 4 offers a deep dive into connected risk. After looking at ways to jump-start connected risk thinking in your organization, I identify key attributes of connected risk thinkers in much the same way I examined the attributes of trusted advisors and agents of change in my previous books. We also take an in-depth look at how technology can evolve from impeding to enabling risk-ready, risk-resilient organizations, and identify the "wow factor" that differentiates connected risk organizations from those still on the journey.

We conclude our journey in **Part 5** by shifting our glance forward. This includes sharing strategies for continuous risk monitoring, a critical component in attaining risk resilience, as well as a connected risk maturity model that will enable you to pinpoint where your organization is on the journey. Finally, we explore the future of risk management, and why all the key players must be connected risk agents of change in achieving resilience and seizing opportunities in the face of uncertainty—not only for their organizations, but for their professions.

In the era of permacrisis, our risk management platforms are burning. As with any burning platform, we need fire extinguishers in a hurry. Connected risk not only helps us navigate the smoke-induced uncertainty engulfing our organizations, but also positions us for the value creation essential for ensuring their future prosperity. Let's approach the fire together and begin our connected risk journey.

Part 1

The Era of Permacrisis

CHAPTER 1

Risk Management in the Modern Age

When I began my internal audit career almost five decades ago, words like *risk* and *risk management* were not part of the profession's lexicon. We tended to audit based on cycles and schedules that were not necessarily linked to risk. As my career progressed and the profession matured, I began to appreciate that organizations must take risks to succeed, either accepting or mitigating those risks.

As an internal auditor, I came to value my role in providing assurance when it came to risk management. Crucially, I grew to understand that without effective risk management, organizations often fail to achieve their objectives.

Internal auditors began focusing on risk as a guiding factor in audit planning and resource allocation in the late 1990s. We started experimenting with risk assessments as part of audit planning, and I prepared my first formal risk assessment during that time.

As I recalled in 2014's *Lessons Learned on The Audit Trail*, I still remember how proud I felt when—in 1999, while serving as assistant inspector general for audit at the U.S. Postal Service (USPS)—the inspector general and I documented our view on the USPS' risks on the literal back of a napkin. We were on our way to an international postal conference in China, and at the time that cocktail napkin risk assessment was a bona fide leading practice.

Less than three years later, what was considered a leading practice became mandatory under The Institute of Internal Auditors' (IIA's) 2002 International Professional Practices Framework (IPPF) for internal audit: a periodic risk assessment was to serve as the basis for formulating an annual internal audit plan.

All this to say, while effective risk management has always been integral to organizational success, it didn't ascend to a formal discipline until the 2000s. "Risk" and "risk management" were still nascent concepts, but the word "risk" was now a significant part of the conversation as leading organizations began devoting time and resources to understanding and mitigating risks.

The Committee of Sponsoring Organizations of the Treadway Commission's (COSO's) Enterprise Risk Management framework—considered an authority on risk management for more than 20 years—defines *risk* as "the possibility that events will occur and affect the achievement of objectives," and the purpose of risk management as "creating, preserving, and realizing value."[1] These baseline definitions can serve as touchstones during this book's explorations. But the crucial overarching context is that risk itself is constantly evolving, and today's organizations are operating in a very different risk landscape. Risk velocity and volatility have become far more dramatic in the first half of the 2020s, such that even effective risk management programs are being seriously taxed in the current environment.

These risk conditions are eroding the health, resilience, relevance, and value-creation potential of our organizations. We must find a more sustainable path forward.

Chapters 2 and 3 will take an in-depth look at how these conditions emerged, and their ramifications for how modern organizations chart a strategic course to optimize outcomes and increase resilience. First, it's helpful to set the stage by understanding how views on risk and risk management have evolved. We can't grasp how to "fix" risk management without examining why, how, and for what purposes the discipline of risk management emerged and matured.

The Evolution of Risk Management

The value of risk management is now well understood in many organizations, given its clear benefits for improving decision-making, enhancing resilience, enabling growth, reducing losses, improving resource allocation, and more. When ERM was first being discussed seriously and openly in the late 1990s and early 2000s, however, organizations understandably had questions. Foremost among them: "Is ERM just more alphabet soup 'consultant speak'?"

Risk management needed to define its purpose and affirm its value, and organizations needed guidance to make sense of risk management in the context of their businesses. To that end, organizations like COSO and the International Organization for Standardization (ISO) developed frameworks and guidelines for evaluating risk management and discerning how it should function in different contexts. The evolution of these frameworks illustrates how risk management has advanced over the decades—and illuminates our current questions.

The COSO ERM—Integrated Framework

The roots of COSO's "ERM—Integrated Framework" can be traced back to the desire to understand, detect, and prevent fraudulent financial reporting.

A series of high-profile financial reporting frauds in the late 1970s and early 1980s meant that organizations and regulators were increasingly eager to prevent such incidents in the future. The National Commission on Fraudulent Financial Reporting—an initiative led by James C. Treadway, Jr., a former commissioner of the U.S. Securities and Exchange Commission (SEC) and thus commonly referred to as the "Treadway Commission"—was established in 1985 and jointly sponsored by The IIA, American Institute of Certified Public Accountants (AICPA), Financial Executives International (FEI), American Accounting Association (AAA), and Institute of Management Accountants (IMA). The Treadway Commission's 1987 report emphasized the downstream impacts of financial reporting frauds.

> When fraudulent financial reporting occurs, serious consequences ensue. The damage that results is widespread, with a sometimes devastating ripple effect. Those affected may range from the immediate victims—the company's stockholders and creditors—to the more remote—those harmed when investor confidence in the stock market is shaken. Between these two extremes, many others may be affected: employees who suffer job loss or diminished pension fund value; depositors in financial institutions; the company's underwriters, auditors, attorneys, and insurers; and even honest competitors whose reputations suffer by association.[2]

In other words—viewed through the lens of our modern definitions of "risk" and "risk management"—the commission assessed that financial reporting fraud risk could severely jeopardize an organization's objectives of creating, preserving, and realizing value for an expansive range of stakeholders.

The report also stated, "No company, regardless of size or business, is immune from the possibility that fraudulent financial reporting will occur. That possibility is inherent in doing business." The report thus issued a series of recommendations focused on preventing fraudulent financial reporting, one of which was that "its sponsoring organizations cooperate in developing additional, integrated guidance on internal controls."[3]

The commission (today known as COSO) ultimately did just that, issuing its first internal control model in 1992. The initial COSO "Internal Control—Integrated Framework" took the form of a pyramid with five interconnected, iterative components. As described in a 2011 paper in the *Journal of Academic and Business Ethics*:

- The pyramid's base was the organization's **control environment,** "the enterprise's people, specifically their integrity, ethical values, and competence, and their work environment."
- The succeeding layer, **risk assessment,** "requires implementation of mechanisms to identify, analyze, and manage risks that threaten to prevent the company from achieving its objectives."
- Next, **control activities** constitute the "policies and procedures... designed and executed to address the risks identified by management in the risk assessment level."
- Lastly, **monitoring** denotes how "the entire internal control process must be monitored and modified when the need arises," and **information and communication** represents "the capture and transfer of data needed by the business to conduct and control operations."[4]

This early model undoubtedly played a role in the emerging leading practice of using risk assessments to guide internal audit planning. Nevertheless, the 1992 model did not initially have a massive impact until it exploded in popularity following the Sarbanes-Oxley Act (SOX) a decade later.

With the help of PricewaterhouseCoopers (PwC) and an advisory council made up of thought leaders from accounting, academia, and business,

COSO released the "Enterprise Risk Management—Integrated Framework" in 2004.[5] As it did with the internal control framework, COSO illustrated its ERM framework with a graphic: a multidimensional cube that illustrated the relationships between the internal environment, objective setting, event identification, risk assessment, risk response, control activities, information and communication, and monitoring. COSO's 2004 framework advanced the ERM body of knowledge by highlighting how risk management is integrated with strategy and performance, including operations, compliance, and reporting, as well as how views on risk and risk management may vary at different levels of the organization (i.e., entity-level, division, business unit, subsidiary).

Unfortunately, the COSO ERM framework wasn't widely appreciated or adopted at the time. I believe this was partly due to the framework's issuance shortly after the business community became totally immersed in the urgent need to enhance internal controls over financial reporting, given the fallout from the Enron and WorldCom scandals and the subsequent passage of SOX in 2002. I have always thought it was ironic that the connection between risks and controls was lost on many at the time. After all, the urgent need to design and implement internal controls over financial reporting was a direct outcome of the risk. It was as if people couldn't see the proverbial forest for the trees.

The 2004 COSO ERM framework may have been ahead of its time, but its time did come. The great financial crisis of 2007–2008 made the consequences of ineffective risk management abundantly clear. It was largely due to the financial crisis—which constituted a failure of risk management itself in the U.S. banking system—that the credibility of risk management advanced several steps forward, becoming seen as an important discipline and differentiator in protecting, creating, and sustaining organizational value.

After all, organizations don't exist simply to protect value, which is how most organizations thought of controls. They exist to create and realize value, no matter the sector, geography, or business strategy.

As The IIA's CEO, I joined COSO's board in 2009, serving for more than 10 years. It was a dynamic period for COSO: we updated the 1992 internal control framework in 2013, and the ERM framework in 2017. The updated ERM framework reflected a maturing appreciation for the role risk management plays in organizational success. Carol Fox, former VP, Director, and Chair at the Risk and Insurance Management Society, highlighted the key changes in a 2018 article in *Risk Management* magazine.[6]

- **Revised definition of risk:** Whereas the 2004 version said that "Risk is the possibility that an event will occur and adversely affect the achievement of objectives," the 2017 version indicated that "Risk is the possibility that events will occur and affect the achievement of objectives." Note the removal of "adversely," because risk isn't solely focused on protecting value.
- **Expanded vision of the purpose of effective ERM:** The 2017 version now pointed to a purpose of "managing risk in creating, preserving, and realizing value." The executive summary described the updated framework as (1) more clearly connecting ERM with the expectations of various stakeholders, (2) positioning risk in the context of the organization's performance (rather than as an isolated exercise), (3) enabling organizations to better anticipate and get ahead of risk, with the understanding that change creates the potential for both crises and opportunities, and (4) emphasizing how ERM informs organizational strategy and performance.[7]
- **New visual representation to convey ERM framework:** COSO discarded the cube in favor of a new structure with colorful intertwining ribbons echoing those of a DNA strand. The new visual representation effectively highlights how ERM's interdependent components and principles are embedded across the organization. I will return to this diagram in chapter 8, when I introduce my idea for a new conceptual framework focused on increasing alignment and collaboration between the key risk players.

ISO 31000 Risk Management—Guidelines

COSO, of course, wasn't the only entity working to help organizations understand and apply the principles of effective risk management. The International Organization for Standardization (ISO) first issued its 31000 risk management guidelines in 2009. As the age-old aphorism states, timing is everything; accordingly, ISO 31000:2009—coming out in the middle of the Great Recession, when there was widespread recognition that risk management had failed—was met with widespread acclaim.

ISO was born of a 1946 effort in which delegates from 25 countries met to discuss the future of international standardization. The organization sought to "facilitate the coordination and unification of standards developed by its member bodies, all of which were national standardization entities in their respective countries."[8] In 1947, 67 technical committees were established across different fields with the mandate to develop international standards; nearly 80 years later, ISO standards cover most aspects of technology and business. So, though 31000 is only one standard set among ISO's hundreds, it has proven hugely impactful on the global stage.

In overview, ISO's principles-based risk management framework provides direction around designing, implementing, monitoring, and continually improving organizational risk management, thereby guiding the development of processes, practices, policies, and procedures to support effective risk management. Because ISO is committed to revising all its standards to ensure they remain "relevant, useful tools for the marketplace," ISO published a revision to 31000 in 2018, citing "new challenges faced by business and organizations" such as "the increased complexity of economic systems and emerging risk factors such as digital currency."[9]

While ISO's definition of risk remained the same from the 2009 to the 2018 version—both define risk as "the effect of uncertainty on objectives"—ISO 31000:2018 contained other noteworthy changes. As ISO's executive summary explained, there was now a "greater focus on creating value as the key driver of risk management" and "more strategic guidance...plac[ing] more emphasis on both the involvement of senior management and the integration of risk management into the organization."[10]

Specifically, ISO 31000:2018 provides direction on how organizations can "integrate risk-based decision-making into an organization's governance, planning, management, reporting, policies, values and culture," with an "overarching goal is to develop a risk management culture where employees and stakeholders are aware of the importance of monitoring and managing risk."[11] To that end, ISO added a recommendation that organizations develop a formal statement or policy confirming a commitment to risk management and "assigning authority, responsibility and accountability at the appropriate levels within the organization and ensuring that the necessary resources are allocated to managing risk."[12]

These significant developments encouraged organizations to take a wider view spanning the enterprise. This perspective better spotlighted risks' threats and opportunities, supported more risk-based resource allocation, and helped organizations see the direct link between risk management and improved governance and performance.

Fox's *Risk Management* magazine article (which tracked notable differences in both COSO's 2017 and ISO's 2018 updates) called out another significant revision, writing that "The standard introduces the concept of adapting risk management frameworks to address external and internal changes in addition to including the risk management framework as part of an organization's normal continual improvement processes."[13] These additions are especially critical for enabling effective risk management in the modern age; I'll explore these ideas in greater depth in future chapters.

Changing Stakeholder Expectations

Beyond appreciating how risk management frameworks and guidelines have evolved over the past two decades, it is essential to underscore how stakeholder expectations are evolving.

Risk and assurance teams are, by definition, client-service functions. Our primary clients are our organizations' boards, audit committees, and executive management teams. We must also consider the various "client" stakeholders (e.g., investors, shareholders, customers, employees, regulators, partners) to whom these oversight and leadership functions are beholden.

The key challenge is that our clients' expectations are fluid based on changing circumstances. They necessarily shift alongside variations in the risk environment; organizations' changing strategies, priorities, business models, or risk appetites; the pressures under which they're operating (including changes in the regulatory environment); and other factors. Accordingly, client service is a constantly changing equation wherein clients' satisfaction is a function of their expectations minus their perceptions. If they expected more than they received, they are not satisfied. If they expected less than they received, the level of satisfaction increases accordingly. Understanding how risk management must transform to better meet the needs of the modern age is therefore also a function of understanding, and continually reassessing, how client expectations are changing.

The most consequential expectation to understand at this juncture: today's executives, boards, and audit committees want more from their risk and assurance teams. To make the decisions that will help their organizations become and remain resilient, they need to be more agile. That means they need their internal audit, risk management, compliance, and information security teams to become better at identifying and responding to emerging risks, and continuously monitoring key risks. In short, all of these key risk players must come together to reimagine their approach to risk management.

These key risk teams are often described as the "three lines," denoting the three distinct roles they play relative to risk management: first-line management owns and manages risks and controls; second-line teams (e.g., risk management, compliance, InfoSec) assist with monitoring and oversight of risk management and controls effectiveness; and third-line internal audit provides independent assurance on the effectiveness of risk management and controls. The three lines approach, however, has not consistently supported a holistic approach to ERM.

For too long, many organizations equated ERM with a risk assessment—often a once-a-year exercise. The ERM function (if there was one) was typically staffed by one person or committee. Most likely, that person or committee was also juggling other responsibilities. In many cases, executive sponsorship of ERM was lacking; some leaders saw it simply as a board directive—a box to be checked.

Today's leaders typically know better. In the unprecedented risk environment of the 2020s, such check-the-box approaches will get organizations precisely nowhere. As Peter Bäckman wrote in a 2022 LinkedIn article, "[Twenty-first]-century ERM redefines the value proposition of risk management by elevating its focus from the tactical to the strategic," enabling organizations to plan and execute capacities "for dealing with the risks that matter."[14]

The question we will strive to answer together in this book: how must risk management evolve to meet the needs of this new reality?

A Paradigm Shift Guided by Value Creation

The north star that professionals across all three lines must bear continually in mind: organizations don't exist simply to protect value. You won't achieve the organization's critical goals and objectives simply by protecting the value you already have. The worthier and more essential goal is *creating* value for stakeholders. Stakeholders, which is true regardless of the type of organization or the sector in which it operates. Government entities, for example, also exist to create value for the citizens and taxpayers they serve.

Conventional responses to managing risk and crises are no longer viable. Similarly, much of the conventional thinking about risk is becoming obsolete. Reimagining risk management for the modern age requires creativity, open-mindedness, new ways of thinking, and a revitalized focus on strategy. It also necessitates understanding risk in all its dimensions and adapting our approach to better meet stakeholders' changing needs.

This calls for no less than a true transformation of how organizations approach risk management. The bottom line is that nobody can "do" risk management effectively on their own in this risk environment. Managing risk effectively requires all hands on deck, working together to find new ways to capitalize on our various strengths. We won't be effective in equipping ourselves to meet today's challenges—let alone the risks we don't see coming—if we're not actively sharing perspectives, data, and insights across audit, risk, compliance, and InfoSec teams.

Maintaining risk awareness is becoming ever more critical in today's risk environment. Successfully navigating these uncertain conditions will be no easy feat. A good first step in our journey is to arm ourselves with a clearer understanding of what has transpired—and more important, what we have learned—during the first half of the 2020s.

CHAPTER 2

The Emergence of Permacrisis

Today's risk landscape is so changed, chaotic, and unprecedented that a new term had to be invented to properly describe it: permacrisis. *Collins Dictionary* declared "permacrisis" 2022's "word of the year," defining it as "An extended period of instability and insecurity, especially one resulting from a series of catastrophic events."[1] As Collins Managing Director Alex Beecroft aptly stated, "Language can be a mirror to what is going on in society and the wider world, and this year has thrown up challenge after challenge."[2]

The world has always known crisis, but the 2020s are exposing us to a special kind of chaos. Risk-induced disruption was pervasive within mere days of the dawn of the new decade. We are not operating in normal times, and permacrisis has proven to have an unprecedented ability to destroy value. Accordingly, to understand why our approach to risk management must change, we first need to better understand the new risk landscape we are living in—the landscape of permacrisis.

The first half of the 2020s has entailed a remarkable series of monumentally disruptive risk events. As each new crisis unfolds, none of the previous crises have completely gone away. Before we can diagnose the new crisis, we're onto the next one. As I wrote in a 2023 blog:

> We are in a state of persistent crisis, with no sense of how we'll escape... Risk managers and internal auditors are charged to assess risk and to advise management and the board on the overall effectiveness of the organization's ability to manage risk. In the past, we had confidence that the crises we faced were solvable, finite, intermittent, and sometimes predictable. In a landscape of permacrisis, we find no such confidence.[3]

Indeed, the age of permacrisis is characterized by ever-deepening ambiguity and complexity. We must embrace these challenges as opportunities. In my

"Auditing at the Speed of Risk" seminar, I emphasize a quote from former COSO Chairman, current IIA collaborator, and longtime risk thought leader, Paul Sobel, which perfectly encapsulates our current challenge: "Risks may be unknown, but they're not unknowable." We will explore the realities of permacrisis in this spirit.

The Preface to Permacrisis

At the end of 2019, the world was emerging from a long decade of stagnation.

The global financial crisis and subsequent Great Recession offered difficult lessons, but major reforms in banking and financial regulation followed. When President Barack Obama signed the Dodd-Frank Wall Street Reform and Consumer Protection Act of 2010 (the Dodd-Frank Act) into law, he remarked at the signing ceremony:

> While a number of factors led to such a severe recession, the primary cause was a breakdown in our financial system. It was a crisis born of a failure of responsibility from certain corners of Wall Street to the halls of power in Washington. For years, our financial sector was governed by antiquated and poorly enforced rules that allowed some to game the system and take risks that endangered the entire economy.
>
> Unscrupulous lenders locked consumers into complex loans with hidden costs. Firms like AIG placed massive, risky bets with borrowed money. And while the rules left abuse and excess unchecked, they left taxpayers on the hook if a big bank or financial institution ever failed.[4]

As Federal Reserve Bank Assistant General Counsel, Keith Goodwin, pointed out in the Federal Reserve History article from which I have drawn this quote, one need not agree with Obama's description of these causes to appreciate that it accurately reflects how legislators perceived those causes when they drafted the Dodd-Frank Act. The financial crisis and its downstream impacts laid bare how regulations sometimes fail to keep pace with market innovations and behaviors—and how taxpayers ultimately paid the price.

Organizations moved into the 2010s with a growing appreciation of the importance of risk management, as mentioned in the previous chapter.

However, recovery was slow, and the economy remained weak. Economic growth averaged only about 2 percent in the first four years of recovery, and the unemployment rate remained at historically elevated levels. The Federal Reserve held interest rates exceptionally low, publicly stating their intentions to keep them that way.[5]

Ultimately, the 2010s proved to be the longest economic recovery on record. As a 2019 Reuters article rightly assessed, a soaring stock market, 110 months of uninterrupted job gains, and plummeting unemployment only told part of the story. The wealth gap was growing, job gains were concentrated—between 2010 and 2017, a shocking 40 percent of all new jobs were created in just 20 cities—and a shortage of homes for sale was making the American Dream less and less attainable for much of the population.[6]

Nevertheless, many economists, policymakers, and business and thought leaders (myself included) had an optimistic outlook going into the 2020s. The coming decade seemed to offer so much promise as we regarded our globally connected world through rose-colored glasses. To help illustrate how optimistic I was mere months before COVID:

- My 2019 Audit Beacon blog featuring **general predictions for the 2020s that could profoundly impact our lives** anticipated that several economies would adopt basic or universal income models. I also focused on predictions that China would overtake the U.S. in terms of gross domestic product (GDP) as soon as 2020.[7] Obviously, neither prediction has come to pass.
- My 2019 Audit Beacon blog with **five bold predictions for internal audit in the 2020s** anticipated that internal auditors like myself would finally shed their "bean counter" image, and that the high-profile scandals of the 2010s would heighten awareness among regulators and legislators of the vital role internal audit plays in serving the public interest. I felt this would heighten internal audit's profile, improve corporate reporting on risk management, and ultimately improve overall corporate governance.[8] We're still working on all of this as well.

Prevailing trends and conditions seemed to offer considerable fodder for optimism. A December 2019 CNBC article by author, journalist, and global affairs think tank leader Frederic Kempe highlighted how global prosperity was rising: the Legatum Prosperity Index suggested that global well-being had hit its highest levels ever, with prosperity improving in more than 88 percent of the countries represented in its surveys. World Bank data showed that the share of the global population in extreme poverty was at the lowest level ever recorded. Half of the world's population now lived in democracies and could be considered "middle class." There were rumblings that artificial intelligence (AI) could be harnessed to improve health care and tackle climate change. Kempe's article closed by quoting the Dalai Lama: "Choose to be optimistic. It feels better."[9]

Enter the Pandemic

Almost immediately, the switch was flipped. The arrival of the COVID-19 pandemic in early 2020—the worst pandemic the world has seen in at least a century—forever changed what we thought we knew about the future.

COVID-19 exposed once and for all how interconnected and interdependent our world has become. Risk-disruptive events can no longer be contained. Everything connects with everything. While we'd largely been viewing this interconnection as a positive, COVID-19 demonstrated how these events can quickly locate the path of least resistance and make their way around the world, leaving an ever-widening swath of devastation in their wake.

The health impact was the world's first focus, as populations struggled to understand transmission and determine how best to stop the spread of the deadly disease while simultaneously treating the fast-growing ranks of those infected—and acknowledging how very many were quickly dying. *Nature*'s April 2020 analysis of COVID-19's first three months assessed that the pandemic had already spread to almost every region of the globe.[10] *Euronews* reported in April 2020 that more than 3.9 billion people—half of the world's population—were on lockdown, having been asked or ordered to stay at home to prevent the spread of COVID-19.[11]

Ultimately, the pandemic resulted in the most simultaneous shutdowns in history.

What would be the economic impact of shutting down the world? How should governments come to the aid of their people and their businesses? When should the shutdowns be relaxed, and with what protocols in place?

What would come next? Because answers were unknowable, governments and health organizations worldwide simply made their best efforts. Dozens of countries funded economic recovery and stimulus programs, each investing trillions. Economies bounced hard, but as if on a trampoline, emerging with such momentum that many quickly overheated.

Simultaneously, the pandemic had already severely disrupted global supply chains, workplaces, and talent pools. Further, with so much of the world staying home, consumer demand shifted from services to goods, significantly increasing inflationary pressures on goods. In their analysis of the causes of pandemic-era inflation in the U.S., former U.S. Federal Reserve Chair Ben Bernanke and French economist and author Olivier Blanchard assessed that shocks to food and energy prices, as well as the combined effects of shortages caused by supply chain disruptions and increased demand for durables, were the primary contributors to inflation between 2020 and 2022.[12] Whatever the case, the average rate of inflation in the U.S. reached a 40-year peak in mid-2022.[13]

An Interconnected Chain

Countless more unanticipated risks materialized from 2021 through early 2022. The Great Resignation—largely an American malaise—saw employees voluntarily leaving their jobs, citing health and safety concerns, low pay, general dissatisfaction, lack of benefits, limited opportunity, and a lack of flexibility or work-life balance. My own decision to step away from The IIA CEO role after 12 years was influenced by a desire for a change of scenery in the wake of the pandemic. Though the trend peaked in late 2021, its legacy lingers; we'll return to these impacts in chapter 5.

Then, just when countries began to imagine they had COVID-19 under control and thus could shift their focus to managing macroeconomic pressures—Russia invaded Ukraine in February 2022, making Europe the site of the region's most significant war in 80 years.

Beyond the loss of life, forced displacement of millions, and profound destruction of infrastructure, this seismic event unleashed a whole new set of risks: intense supply chain disruptions, including to the global energy market and food supply. Deeply strained international relations. Sudden pressure to pull money and operations out of Russia, such that many organizations chose to divest, move, or close Russian offices. Displacement of highly skilled sectors of the Russian workforce, many of whom worked for organizations based elsewhere in the world. Increased cybersecurity threats from Russia. Heightened concerns about the security of nuclear power plants and even the prospect of nuclear conflict. Uneasiness and uncertainty on a global scale.

As 2022 wore on, regulators and organizations in the U.S. also had fresh concerns at home, with a banking system again under pressure. As the Federal Reserve raised interest rates in their attempts to combat rising inflation, government bonds decreased in value. Accordingly, as Pew Research documented, Silicon Valley Bank's (SVB's) large holdings of government bonds lost value while startup funding was drying up and more SVB customers were withdrawing their money. After SVB sold off its entire bond portfolio to shore up its balance sheet, customers panicked and sped up withdrawals, ultimately leading to the bank's failure in early 2023.[14]

SVB was only the first bank to fall. Signature Bank failed less than 48 hours later, and First Republic Bank the following month. This seeming contagion of bank failures shook consumer confidence in the stability of the banking system and put the Federal Reserve under renewed pressure to bolster an ailing system. The nation fluctuated between worrying about inflation to watching for signs of recession.

By the end of 2023, however, the banking crisis and recessionary worries were again secondary, when the most violent war to break out in 50 years erupted in the Middle East. As with the Russia-Ukraine war, the conflict between Hamas and Israel has had countless direct and indirect impacts felt the world over. The undeniable humanitarian crisis means pressure is mounting on global governments to intervene. Whatever the eventual outcome and aftereffects, the Israel-Hamas war has created yet another fissure through which the world is experiencing increasing polarization.

Over this same period, the use of generative AI was increasing exponentially. ChatGPT, which enjoyed its splashy public debut in November 2022, brought AI firmly into the limelight. Individuals and organizations began diving in wholeheartedly to explore AI's potential—often without assessing the risks and without putting appropriate governance in place. We'll examine AI's increasingly earthshaking impact in more detail as we proceed.

What's more, this same time period has also seen a rapid expansion of regulatory frameworks and requirements in areas such as data privacy, cybersecurity, and environmental, social, and governance (ESG). As we'll explore further in chapter 4, this proliferation of new requirements increases the burden and complexity of compliance, the potential risks and costs associated with noncompliance, and the strain on organizations' already challenged risk management resources.

This interconnected chain of risks and crises is without end. It encircles the world, pulling ever tighter.

These volatile moments combine. They become a month, a year, an era. The era of permacrisis demands we focus on strategically positioning ourselves and our organizations not only for success, but sheer survival.

The New Reality of Risk Management

The first half of the 2020s have taught us a profound and unforgettable lesson in the ripple effects of risk, and ultimately the speed of risk and value destruction. While a few pages of narrative can only cover so much, it nevertheless paints a compelling picture of a risk landscape entirely reshaped. While the world contained the worst of the pandemic itself, the pandemic unleashed forces no one envisioned and generated downstream impacts we will feel for years to come. Alongside these effects, unforeseen geopolitical developments have created a risk environment of extraordinary uncertainty.

This hard lesson on risks' far-reaching impacts embodies the new reality of risk management: organizations must become better at understanding, monitoring, and responding to the chain of risks as it unfurls. What potential threats and opportunities are created by each new crisis? When a significant disruptive risk event occurs, how can we plan for the downstream impacts? Perhaps most pressingly, how can we hope to anticipate the risks that will be unleashed next?

No crisis will be like the last one. There is no playbook. Instead of trying to write new playbooks that will quickly become outdated, we must approach the problem differently. To understand how, we can begin by learning from the experiences of organizations for which risk management proved pivotal during the first half of the 2020s.

CHAPTER 3

The Speed of Risk and Value Destruction

A uniquely unpredictable risk environment marked the first half of the 2020s with risk velocity and volatility increasing faster than ever before. We have entered unknown territory, but we must find our way through regardless. Preparing for a successful journey warrants a deeper dive on the speed of risk and value destruction, granting us a more complete view of the realities of doing business in this environment.

An organization's ability to withstand chaotic conditions often comes down to risk management. While we have seen a high mortality rate for many legacy companies—S&P Global reported a total of 642 bankruptcy filings in 2023, the highest since 2010[1]—others are thriving well beyond expectations. This chapter explores several of these stories, putting the spotlight on the role of risk management in each organization's demise or triumph. To properly set the stage, however, we must first paint in the backdrop: the multitude of powerful factors driving risk velocity and volatility.

Factors That Drive Risk Velocity and Volatility

When speaking about today's risk environment I often talk about *RV*², my shorthand for expressing the "compounding impact of risk velocity and volatility." As we strive to understand organizations' economic, environmental, geopolitical, societal, technological, financial, operational, and strategic risks, it's helpful to understand the many factors that can drive each.

Risk velocity is the speed at which risks change or evolve within a system, organization, or project. Figure 3-1 illustrates several of the foremost factors.

Figure 3-1
Factors Driving Risk Velocity

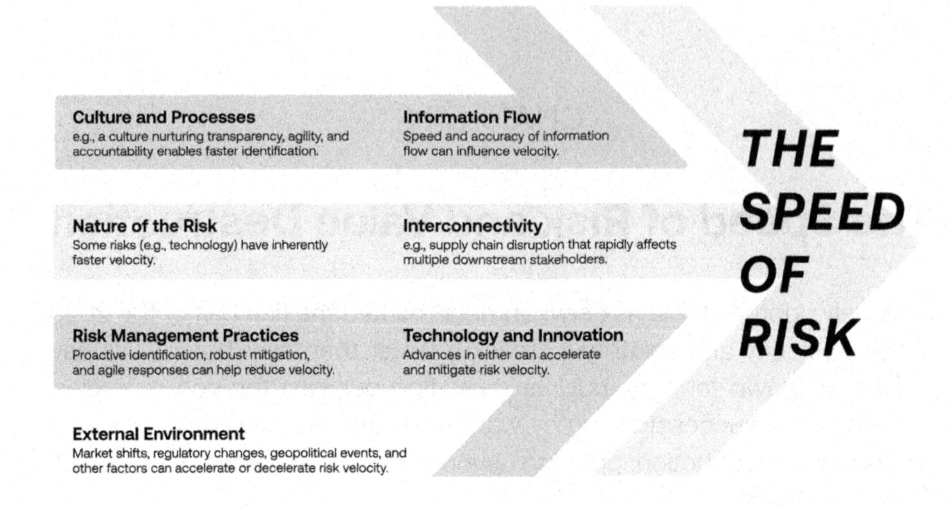

Culture and Processes
e.g., a culture nurturing transparency, agility, and accountability enables faster identification.
Information Flow
Speed and accuracy of information flow can influence velocity.
Nature of the Risk
Some risks (e.g., technology) have inherently faster velocity.
Interconnectivity
e.g., supply chain disruption that rapidly affects multiple downstream stakeholders.
Risk Management Practices
Proactive identification, robust mitigation, and agile responses can help reduce velocity.
Technology and Innovation
Advances in either can accelerate and mitigate risk velocity.
External Environment
Market shifts, regulatory changes, geopolitical events, and other factors can accelerate or decelerate risk velocity.
THE SPEED OF RISK

Risk volatility is the degree of variability or fluctuation in the level of risk within a system or environment over time. Figure 3-2 depicts the primary factors driving risk volatility.

Figure 3-2
Factors Driving Risk Volatility

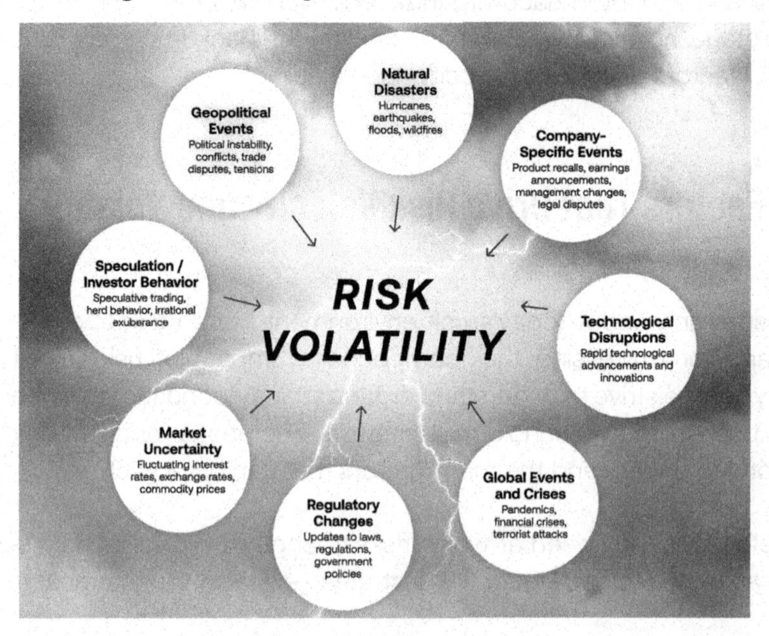

Using RV^2 to Drive Planning and Monitoring

Efforts to understand the driving factors behind risk velocity and volatility are akin to predicting the weather. We cannot wait until we hear the thunder or see the storm surge to assess that storms are coming. We must instead become adept at monitoring and interpreting changing weather patterns, learning to identify the early warning signs of an approaching storm.

I have often talked about internal auditors and risk managers as the "meteorologists" of corporate risk management. Just as meteorologists bring their expertise to understand the Doppler radar, satellite, and other technologies they use to detect and monitor the approach of hurricanes, tornadoes, blizzards, and other storms, audit and risk professionals must pair risk acumen with monitoring strategies to see and understand the early warning signs of emerging risks. In both cases, the goal is to anticipate the risk of incipient "storms" far beyond the visible horizon.

Permacrisis is the most immense and unpredictable storm pattern we have ever experienced. That does not excuse us from doing our best to anticipate what's coming next.

Granted, it is no small feat to get one's head around the many diverse factors driving RV^2. At minimum, understanding the categories can help organizations direct monitoring efforts and plan accordingly. Chapter 4 references several external sources that can become part of monitoring, enabling timely warnings on key risks and drivers. Chapter 13 explores specific continuous risk monitoring strategies.

The crux of the matter is that understanding permacrisis' incredible potential for value destruction—and value creation—requires accounting for risk velocity and volatility. But broad categories and weather analogies can only take us so far. Accordingly, we need to examine how specific organizations weathered the storms of permacrisis. What can we learn about the speed of risk and value destruction from looking at the permacrisis of the past five years in more detail?

Case Studies in Value Destruction

Countless organizations did not survive the risk-induced disruption of the first half of the 2020s. In many cases, pandemic shutdowns were a significant factor. The hospitality industry took a beating, with restaurants suffering or shuttering, tours and travel abruptly canceled, cruises metamorphosing into quarantines, and hotels desperate for occupants conducting mass layoffs and, in some cases, closing for good. Theaters, museums, and other entertainment venues were forced to close, with legions of artists, performers, and crews suddenly unemployed. Unsurprisingly, shopping malls and retailers were hard-hit. Retailers like JCPenney, J.Crew, and Tailored Brands (owner of Men's Wearhouse and Jos. A. Bank), for example, suffered greatly when the working world stayed home and demand for workplace fashion plummeted. Online shopping had already dented these retailers' fortunes and futures, but it was the economic impact of the pandemic that led all three to file for bankruptcy[2]. (Note: All have subsequently emerged from bankruptcy.)

The driving factors behind other organizations' failures, however, are more murky and mixed. As reflected in the banking industry failures mentioned in the previous chapters, it almost always comes down to risk management. We've chosen four illustrative cases to highlight.

Bed Bath & Beyond

Bed Bath & Beyond, of course, is another retailer that famously didn't survive the pandemic. But its risk management failures spanned decades before it filed for bankruptcy in April 2023 and announced its intent to close all remaining locations.

Founded in 1971, Bed Bath & Beyond was a home furnishing superpower for much of its 52 years. After the company went public in 1992, as reported by CBS News, it "had a 15-year run of earnings that met or beat Wall Street expectations."[3] It counted itself among the fortunate ranks of the Fortune 500 and Forbes Global 2000.

By the early 2000s, however, online shopping was taking off. E-commerce websites like Amazon promised lower prices, more options, and the option to buy (and return) your bath mat or blender from the comfort of your own couch. But as online shopping continued growing exponentially, Bed Bath & Beyond was slow to act. As a post-mortem by From assessed:

> While the company took some early strides toward digital—they launched their website in 1999—they didn't make substantial investments to deliver a superior online experience for customers. They failed to foresee how much of an impact digital would have on their industry.
>
> Bed Bath & Beyond co-founder Warren Eisenberg admitted as much: "If you told me that some of my grandchildren will get all their dresses on the Internet, I would say, 'People like to go out and shop. It's a social thing to do.' We didn't realize fast enough how the Internet would have such a major effect on retail."[4]

In fact, Bed Bath & Beyond continued to acquire more brick-and-mortar retailers, including Harmon Face Values, Buy Buy Baby, and Cost Plus World Market. According to Statista, Bed Bath & Beyond peaked at more than 1,550 stores worldwide in 2018.[5]

As CBS News' rundown reported, a former Bed Bath & Beyond CEO (who had led the company since 2003) was part of the problem. He was unapologetically "old-school" and unwilling to adjust his tactics or strategy. By the time Bed Bath & Beyond had installed a new CEO in 2019, the company had fallen too far behind to catch up. The new CEO made big moves, including redesigning the stores' look and reducing the amount of merchandise sitting on shelves. He also initiated an astronomical USD 625 million stock buyback that spooked the company's suppliers, who feared the company wouldn't have enough cash to pay them. Vendors scaled back their business, such that Bed Bath & Beyond's remaining customers found little merchandise to buy and plenty of reasons to be unhappy.[6]

That all happened, however, in the two years *before* the pandemic. When the pandemic hit and demand for home furnishings spiked, very few people chose to go to Bed Bath & Beyond's subpar retail website.

There is, of course, more to the story. As a Wharton Business School article detailed, the new CEO experimented with private-label products—a strategy that had served him well during his tenure at Target Corporation—but they were of poor quality with a marketing campaign to match. He also reduced and tightened restrictions on the company's famous, much-beloved coupons. As Wharton marketing professor Barbara Kahn explained:

> Consumers went to BBB looking for the national brands and just didn't recognize or trust the private brands. Supply chain issues during the pandemic didn't help. BBB also got rid of their coupons, and using these coupons drove consumer traffic to the store. Without those coupons as a trigger to go shopping, foot traffic dropped...While the private brand strategies and lessened reliance on couponing were no doubt designed to improve margins, they instead lowered sales.[7]

Bed Bath & Beyond also suffered from controversial governance before the departure of the previous CEO. Media reports noted that Bed Bath & Beyond had acquired two retailers founded by children of company founders, and a group of activist investors called out the acquisitions in 2019 as nepotism and poor business practices. The challenge led to five directors stepping down, restructuring of the board, and the CEO's resignation.

All of these risk management failures and more combined to lead to the retailer's eventual bankruptcy. In 2020—the pandemic's first year—it began selling off subsidiaries and closing hundreds of stores. The bleeding continued. The company replaced the new CEO, and announced more layoffs and store closings.

Online retailer Overstock.com acquired the company's intellectual property assets, including its trademarks, in a bankruptcy auction. The day the acquisition was announced, Overstock's stock rose more than 17 percent.[8] In other words, Bed Bath & Beyond—the big-box retailer that failed to thrive largely because of its lack of investment in establishing an e-commerce presence—"survives" today as an e-commerce site.

WeWork

WeWork filed for Chapter 11 bankruptcy protection in November 2023. The once-promising contender fell hard. As Reuters reported, the Silicon Valley-based WeWork was at one point the most valuable startup in the U.S., worth an estimated USD 47 billion, with enthusiastic investors that included SoftBank, Benchmark, and JPMorgan Chase.[9]

WeWork's business model was disruptive when it debuted in 2010. The company sought to revolutionize the office market. They took long-term leases on large office properties and rented the space out to multiple businesses via shorter, more flexible leases than traditional office leasing permitted. The proposition was attractive to both small and large businesses:

small businesses appreciated how easy it was to scale or move office space as they grew, and larger businesses enjoyed operating without the burdens of property ownership and having greater overall flexibility on terms.

A promising business model indeed. So what went wrong? WeWork's demise is primarily a story of strategic risk management failure—on the part of both WeWork itself and its investors. Reuters' analysis quoted investor Steve Clayton, who bluntly assessed, "The company was the product of a boom, and during booms, investors ignore the flashing warning lights. 'Charismatic CEO' is a term that should strike fear into any investor's heart."[10]

The "charismatic CEO" in question brought unfettered ambition, eccentric leadership, and lapses in corporate governance (including reported conflicts of interest such as leasing buildings he owned to WeWork, firing employees without cause, and more), ultimately leading to his firing in 2019. He may have charmed investors, but he and his leadership team lacked a long-term strategic plan for filling the space the company had very aggressively leased across the globe. The CEO talked of expanding the business to residential housing and schools. However, WeWork's projections were overly optimistic, it lacked a path to profitability, and its presentations to investors misrepresented the nature of the business and its profits.[11]

The company was overvalued, overextended, and losing money fast, facts that were already well-known to many. In 2017, the *Wall Street Journal* called out the "$20 Billion Startup Fueled by Pixie Dust,"[12] and you might have assumed smart investors would stay away. They did not. While the failed 2019 initial public offering was a debacle and key investors—including SoftBank—did subsequently push the CEO out, SoftBank continued to invest billions.

Then came the pandemic. As NPR reported, by 2021, the company had enlisted traditional real estate executives to run the company.[13] Demand for office space was plunging post-COVID, but WeWork's clients were also simply canceling agreements. Regrettably, the company had already leased so much office space worldwide, and much of it sat empty. As debt piled up, cash ran out. SoftBank initiated a bailout, but as interest rates rose, borrowing became more expensive, and WeWork continued to burn through cash, there was no way out but bankruptcy—which may be SoftBank's best hope for recouping any of its lost billions.[14]

Peloton

Fitness company Peloton has experienced both towering highs and plunging lows in recent years. Once dubbed "the Apple of Fitness," Peloton enjoyed a steep growth curve early on, reaching unicorn status with a valuation of USD 1.25 billion in 2017.[15] Now, the company's very future is in question.

As CNBC's Make It explained, in 2011, one of Peloton's co-founders was a busy executive at Barnes & Noble when he pitched a former colleague (who became another co-founder) on the idea that "technology could make it possible for time-strapped people to get the full experience of working out in a high-end studio cycling class in their homes." He himself was frustrated at his inability to fit workouts into his schedule, and the idea for an at-home exercise bike with a screen that live streams cycling classes was born. The pair founded Peloton in 2012 along with three other co-founders; by 2013, they had a prototype, a successful Kickstarter campaign, and growing consumer interest. Sales took off in 2015, and within a few years they had several lucrative funding rounds and a small but passionate legion of Peloton enthusiasts.[16]

The vertically integrated company manufactures its own software and hardware and produces its own virtual classes. Peloton also cultivated a cast of popular cycling instructors who gained loyal followings.

While many people ridiculed the bikes' steep price tag, sales were strong, and the company went public in 2019 with a valuation of USD 8.1 billion. When COVID-19 hit, shutting down gyms and keeping everyone home, sales skyrocketed well beyond expectations. As CNBC reported, Peloton's CEO told employees it was only the beginning, operating with what one former employee described as "blind optimism." Peloton hired aggressively while developing new products and paying exorbitant costs to get bikes delivered regardless of the pandemic's hurdles, at times spending nearly $500 per final mile delivery. Peloton said its sales surged 232 percent to USD 757.9 million in November 2020 compared to the prior year.[17]

Unfortunately, supply chain disruptions meant they couldn't keep up with demand—or quality. Deliveries were delayed for months, and bikes that were delivered often suffered from technical issues. Peloton invested USD 100 million in shipping solutions in December 2020, and USD 400 million in a massive Ohio factory meant to shore up manufacturing in May 2021. But the company was losing money fast, and as vaccines became available, demand dropped. CNBC quoted a former Peloton designer who said, "I think all of us were drunk on the growth that Covid brought, and no one paused to say like, hey, maybe this is a game of musical chairs, and what happens when the music stops?"[18]

At the same time, Peloton's treadmills were causing sustained injuries to people and pets, including fractured bones and burns. One child died after being pulled under a treadmill. The U.S. Consumer Product Safety Commission warned people to stop using the product, and Peloton initially rejected the commission's request to recall the products. Ultimately, the company did recall the treadmills and issue refunds, but its reputation suffered.

Peloton laid off 2,800 employees in February 2022 and its CEO—Peloton's original visionary—stepped down. Under the direction of a new CEO, the company started testing new pricing structures and subscription models, lowered pricing on both bikes and treadmills, and focused on improving existing hardware. Still, by the end of June 2022, Peloton's full-year net loss reached USD 2.83 billion.[19] In May 2023, the company faced another safety recall—this time on bikes; two months later, the company announced another 800 job cuts and plans to outsource. The new CEO resigned in May 2024, and by June Peloton's market capitalization had declined to USD 1.3 billion.

An enduring lesson from Peloton's story is that success can never be taken for granted. Companies that seize opportunities, disrupt and transform markets, and create extraordinary value in a short period of time can never lose sight of the risks and opportunities that lie ahead. After all, complacency is not a strategy.

FTX

By now, the story of cryptocurrency exchange FTX's rapid rise and equally expedient fall is well-known in most circles. It is also one of the most vivid examples of widespread risk management failures the world has ever witnessed, easily ranking alongside the WorldCom, Enron, and Madoff scandals. Those were seismic events with earth-shaking implications. FTX's stunning collapse illustrates no less.

As of January 2022, FTX was valued at USD 32 billion and regarded as one of the more stable, well-capitalized, and trustworthy crypto firms.[20] Its founder and CEO was 30-year-old Sam Bankman-Fried, a seeming crypto visionary and champion of effective altruism. He donated millions to favorite causes and offered to buy or bail out other struggling crypto firms. He purported to be pro-regulation for crypto.

That pretty picture shattered utterly in November 2022 when crypto-focused news website CoinDesk reported on a leaked FTX balance sheet that revealed the company's true standing. Alameda Research, FTX's crypto trading arm, reported USD 14.6 billion in assets that relied heavily on FTX's own tokens. On November 11, FTX filed for Chapter 11 bankruptcy protection and announced Bankman-Fried's resignation. The very next day, Reuters reported that Bankman-Fried had secretly transferred USD 10 billion in customer funds from FTX to Alameda, and USD 1–2 billion in customer funds were unaccounted for.[21] Another "charismatic CEO" indeed.

John J. Ray III, the restructuring expert charged with managing Enron's and several other high-profile liquidations, was quickly appointed FTX's CEO. His November 17 bankruptcy filing stated, "Never in my career have I seen such a complete failure of corporate control and such a complete absence of trustworthy financial information." A "substantial portion" of FTX's assets were possibly missing or stolen, and the financial statements—prepared by Armanino LLP in the U.S. and Prager Metis for offshore operations—shouldn't be trusted. He described "an absence of independent governance" between FTX and Alameda: "From compromised systems integrity and faulty regulatory oversight abroad, to the concentration of control in the hands of a very small group of inexperienced, unsophisticated, and potentially compromised individuals, this situation is unprecedented."[22]

Anthony Pugliese, CEO of The IIA, and I wrote a January 2023 article sharing FTX's hard lessons.

> The filing and financials revealed a profound disregard for governance underpinned by a culture of smoke, mirrors, and carelessness. Neither FTX nor Alameda had an audit committee, board meetings, or an internal audit function. Employee ranks were rife with conflicts of interest. Alameda reportedly granted massive personal loans to Bankman-Fried and others. A custom-software "backdoor" was used to conceal the misuse of customer funds. Related-party transactions raised countless red flags. Expenses were approved via personalized emojis in online chats. Many communications were set to auto-delete.

> Notably, neither of FTX's external auditors provided an opinion in their audit reports on internal controls over accounting and financial reporting. It's also been reported that Bankman-Fried clung to control to the very end, insisting he could save the company despite mounting evidence to the contrary provided by other FTX officials.
>
> We can try to assess cause and effect. Did FTX's lack of governance or oversight create its toxic company culture? Or was the reverse true? Frankly, in most cases, culture ends up being the determinant. The tail is not supposed to wag the dog, but it often does when it comes to culture. It's the same lesson that Enron, WorldCom, and all those other earth-shaking scandals should've taught us: Good governance doesn't happen if a culture doesn't value it.

Without sound internal controls, FTX's failure was a foregone conclusion. As Pugliese and I concluded, "Even the greatest business strategies and smartest people will fail without a culture that values effective governance, risk management, and controls."[23]

The story of FTX also demonstrates that, as U.S. Attorney General Merrick Garland said in a statement following Bankman-Fried's sentencing, "There are serious consequences for defrauding customers and investors. Anyone who believes they can hide their financial crimes behind wealth and power, or behind a shiny new thing they claim no one else is smart enough to understand, should think twice."[24]

Indeed, when Bankman-Fried had his day in court, he was found guilty of seven fraud and conspiracy counts and sentenced to 25 years of prison.

Case Studies in Value Creation

We have articulated how the speed of risk can contribute to value destruction. Obviously, failing to anticipate and manage risks can impact your bottom line significantly. The speed of risk, however, can also be framed as the speed of opportunities. The circumstances that can lead to one organization's struggles can lead to another organization's chance to shine. In the right hands, the speed of opportunity can combine with effective risk management to create value.

Adaptation has been key for most businesses that have been able to thrive amid permacrisis. These organizations' boards and business leaders learned to read the environment and pivot accordingly. For others, the conditions of permacrisis were simply the right time to make the big bets, even if and when conventional wisdom told them to be cautious. Read on for three examples of companies that were able to turn disruption into monumental opportunities.

Zoom

Zoom was founded in 2011 by CEO Eric Yuan with the goal of "building the best video conferencing solution on the market."[25] Yuan, who had held VP of Engineering roles at Cisco and WebEx for the first part of his career, knew a thing or two about video conferencing. He had been a founding engineer at WebEx; after WebEx was acquired by Cisco, he played a central role in the success of Cisco's Webex collaboration platform (they dropped the capital E). Yuan reportedly pitched Cisco his idea of a more mobile-friendly video conferencing system—and they turned him down.[26] He also felt that existing video conferencing solutions focused on too few use cases.[27] Yuan was confident he could do better, and had the technical expertise and track record to back up his assertions. Further, he was on a stated mission to make people "happy," focused on delighting customers and employees alike.

Yuan left Cisco to pursue his dream, but the company initially had trouble finding investors, who felt the market was saturated. In 2011, Skype had been around for years, Apple had just launched FaceTime, and Cisco's Webex already dominated the office market. But several angel investors—notably including former Cisco and WebEx leaders—were willing to bet on Yuan.[28] He and his 40 engineers spent two years developing the product; Zoom Meetings launched publicly in 2013, followed a year later by the launch of Zoom Chat, Zoom Webinars, and Zoom Rooms. In under six months, Zoom had connected more than 400,000 meetings, 3,500 businesses, and one million customers.[29]

Zoom quickly invested in strategic partnerships with business-to-business (B2B) collaboration software providers and manufacturers to deliver more capabilities. The company's fast growth and well-thought-out user experience attracted more investments and more users. By 2017, Zoom had reached unicorn status with a USD 1 billion valuation. The company launched an app marketplace in 2018 to support new integrations and a cloud telephone service in 2019, further enhancing the work experience and supporting all-around business communications. Zoom's successful 2019 IPO saw its initial price of USD 36 peak at above USD 104 by mid-year.[30]

Over this time, Yuan had been deliberately investing not only in delivering a best-in-class product, but also in building a happy, healthy company culture. An October 2019 Motley Fool article counted 53 uses of the word "happy" or its derivatives in Zoom's S-1 filing before its IPO and further detailed how Zoom's culture of "delivering happiness" had supported its growth.[31] Zoom has been named one of Glassdoor's "Best Places to Work" in 2018, 2019, 2021, and 2022.

Zoom was ready when the pandemic hit, lockdowns commenced, and demand for video conferencing spiked and remained high. The company acted fast to offer help and continue stepping up its game. While Zoom already offered free accounts, in March 2020 Yuan removed time limits for users in affected regions and offered free, unlimited access for public K-12 schools in the U.S., Japan, Italy, and other countries. Over the course of 2020, Zoom made strategic acquisitions (e.g., Keybase, which specializes in end-to-end encryption; Kites, which performs AI-based language translation), opened new R&D and data centers, and launched its "hardware as a service" and "Zoom for Home" products.

The pandemic handed Zoom an easy victory; the company could have sat back, rested on its laurels, and let the profits roll in. Instead, it challenged itself to keep innovating, and offered customers and schools free access. Now, "Zoom" is shorthand for a video call in the same way that "Kleenex" is for tissues.

No company's risk management record is perfect. Some risks don't pan out. In 2023, echoing the widespread layoffs happening in other technology companies, Zoom announced a 15 percent reduction in its workforce. In a statement the day the layoffs were announced, Yuan took accountability—and a truly mammoth pay cut.

> We worked tirelessly and made Zoom better for our customers and users. But we also made mistakes. We didn't take as much time as we should have to thoroughly analyze our teams or assess if we were growing sustainably, toward the highest priorities.

Yuan continued:

> As the CEO and founder of Zoom, I am accountable for these mistakes and the actions we take today—and I want to show accountability not just in words but in my own actions. To that end, I am reducing my salary for the coming fiscal year by 98 percent and foregoing my FY23 corporate bonus. Members of my executive leadership team will reduce their base salaries by 20 percent for the coming fiscal year while also forfeiting their FY23 corporate bonuses.

Zoom took big swings. When it missed, its leaders took accountability and action. Yuan's statement further offered departing employees up to 16 weeks' salary and healthcare coverage, payment of bonuses for FY2023, stock option vesting, and outplacement services (one-on-one coaching, workshops, networking).[32]

In a 2017 interview, Yuan offered "five things I wish someone had told me before I launched my start-up." The list vividly reflects Yuan's commitment to taking the right risks at the right times, investing in happiness and culture, and choosing the right partners for your journey.

1. Although the start-up journey is long and tough, it's also fun and exciting. Don't be afraid to start—just go for it!
2. You don't need to hire the people who are the most qualified on paper; instead you should hire those with self-motivation and a self-learning mentality.
3. Your company's culture is the #1 most important thing to get right. Everything else flows from there.
4. If your employees are not happy, nothing else at your company will go well.
5. Find the investors who want to invest in you, not only in your business.[33]

NVIDIA

NVIDIA began humbly, as a video game chip company brainstormed by three friends over a meal. In 1993, the company's founders—Jensen Huang, Chris Malachowsky, and Curtis Priem—were at a Silicon Valley Denny's when they envisioned building a computer chip that would make realistic 3D graphics possible on personal computers.

As a child, Huang remembers having his first hamburger and milkshake at a Denny's after his family moved to the U.S. from Taiwan. His first job at age 15, as a dishwasher, busboy, and ultimately server, was at another Denny's, and he credits the experience with teaching him the work ethic, humility, and hospitality that has helped him to succeed.[34] It feels fitting that the restaurant that played such a prominent role in Huang's American Dream was also where the idea for NVIDIA was born.

That day in 1993, the founders knew full well that Intel and Advanced Micro Devices (AMD) strongly dominated the U.S. chip sector. However, as NBC News reported, those companies specialized in producing the central processing units (CPUs) that are foundational to basic computing and software processes, while NVIDIA aimed to specialize in graphics processing units (GPUs), which at the time were primarily associated with video games. NBC News encapsulated what happened next.

> But it turns out GPUs are also able to perform calculations concurrently in a way that regular CPUs cannot—making them more energy efficient and better able to handle sophisticated computing demands.
>
> Over time, the other big chip makers began manufacturing their own GPUs to compete—but Nvidia, having enjoyed a first-mover advantage in the space, was where companies began to turn to for GPU needs.
>
> It combined its chips with a suite of accompanying software that programmers simply preferred. Plus, its supply chain allowed it to produce GPUs in larger volumes, faster, and more reliably, than its rivals. For instance, auto companies began turning to Nvidia chips for use in driver-assistance software that must process image information from sensors.[35]

NVIDIA CEO Huang and his co-founders grasped this potential when they founded the company. Focusing on GPUs could enable them to start with the highly profitable video game market, funding their ability to expand NVIDIA's scope over time. It was a risk they could afford to take, given the clear path to early profitability. As Huang explained in 2017:

> We believed this model of computing could solve problems that general-purpose computing fundamentally couldn't. We also observed that video games were simultaneously one of the most computationally challenging problems and would have incredibly high sales volume.

> Those two conditions don't happen very often. Video games was our killer app—a flywheel to reach large markets funding huge R&D to solve massive computational problems.[36]

Indeed, NVIDIA succeeded in pioneering a new way to accelerate computing while achieving greater sustainability through massive energy savings. As detailed by NVIDIA, the company's global ecosystem now spans 4.5 million developers, 40,000 companies, and more than 3,300 applications. It is responsible for much of the infrastructure powering the world's AI and machine learning models: ChatGPT is powered by an NVIDIA supercomputer, and partnerships with Amazon, Google, Microsoft, and Oracle are enabling NVIDIA to bring state-of-the-art capabilities to thousands of organizations. NVIDIA's full-stack autonomous driving platform supports both cars and data centers. The company has also developed an industrial digitalization platform that "builds virtual representations of physical things and assets—creating digital twins and connecting digital and physical worlds," helping organizations optimize assets in the metaverse before deploying changes. The list goes on and on, powering everything from cryptocurrency mining to design and coding software to AI applications across climate research, healthcare, and beyond.[37] The potential market for NVIDIA is essentially limitless.

Of course, NVIDIA also delivered on its original objective of reinventing computer graphics, making video games look more beautiful and realistic than ever. However, it was the transformation from a "video game chip company" to an enabler of AI and industrial digitalization that gained the attention of investors. As *CIO* reported:

> It was when Nvidia reported strong results for the three months to April 30, 2023, and forecast its sales could jump by 50 percent in the following fiscal quarter, that its stock market valuation soared, catapulting it into the exclusive trillion-dollar club alongside well-known tech giants Alphabet, Amazon, Apple, and Microsoft. The once-niche chipmaker, now a Wall Street darling, was becoming a household name.[38]

The AI revolution is just getting started; demand for NVIDIA's products will only grow. In February 2024, NVIDIA surpassed Apple to become the second-largest publicly traded company in the U.S. by market capitalization (USD 3 trillion), behind only Microsoft. Apple ultimately regained top spot, but NVIDIA's meteoric rise remains notable. Plus, NVIDIA has achieved all of this while building a robust company culture: it has been named among Glassdoor's "Best Places to Work" and Fortune's "Best Companies to Work For" since 2017.

Along the path, Huang has retained his signature balance of drive and humility, earning the reputation as a hands-on boss willing to take on anything. As he told a room full of Stanford graduate students in 2024, "No task is beneath me because, remember, I used to be a dishwasher [and] I used to clean toilets. I've cleaned more toilets than all of you combined."[39]

Huang is playing a long game. He and his leadership team built a strategy that uses a platform approach to enable and support scalable growth across multiple markets, including gaming, AI, crypto, automotive, industrial digitalization, and health care. NVIDIA is thinking big while ensuring sustainability.

Figma

Figma, a collaborative web application for designing user interfaces and prototypes, is a different kind of story. Sure, Figma also grew from a "big idea." But its young founders did not initially understand how revolutionary the company and its product would be. They certainly did not foresee that, a mere 10 years down the road, Adobe would agree to acquire Figma for USD 20 billion—and later that year, facing antitrust concerns and reviews by the U.S. Department of Justice and European Commission, the companies would be forced to abandon the merger.

Per the terms of the original deal, Adobe must pay Figma a "reverse termination fee" of USD 1 billion in cash. As you consider that figure, understand that Figma remains one of Adobe's competitors. But we're getting ahead of ourselves.

Co-founders Dylan Field and Evan Wallace were computer science students at Brown University in 2011 when they began experimenting with design tools built for the web. *The Brown Daily Herald* reported that Field won a grant of USD 100,000 from the prestigious Thiel Fellowship in 2012, leaving Brown to work on the startup's product. At the time, Adobe's Photoshop software—which carried a substantial price tag and learning curve—was the dominant graphic-editing tool. Field and Wallace sought to "make it so that anyone can be creative by creating free, simple, creative tools in a browser."[40]

Wallace joined Field in California following his graduation from Brown. The young founders spent three years quietly building the product, launching it as a free, invite-only beta in 2015. A *TechCrunch* article that year called out the worthy challenge to Adobe presented by Figma's "browser-based alternative to Adobe's desktop software," quoting Field as saying that Adobe "doesn't understand collaboration," and that the Adobe Creative Cloud is "really cloud in name only." The article concluded of Field, "You might mistake it as naive arrogance, but his youthful confidence is what it takes to battle the design Goliath."[41]

Figma launched publicly in 2016, the first collaborative, web-based design platform offering "multiplayer functionality." Often described as "Google Docs for design," Figma's "superpower"—as Field reflected in a 2017 blog—was that it gave teams a single source of truth shareable via URL, "abolishing the complex workflow previously required for syncing design assets and ensuring everyone on a product team is working with the latest file."[42] By solving persistent problems around communication, version control, efficiency, approvals, and handoffs, it effectively revolutionized design workflows. It also made design accessible to more people than ever before: to this day, anyone can try Figma for free.

Not everyone was thrilled with Figma's collaborative model. In 2020, Field retrospectively wrote:

> When my co-founder Evan and I launched Figma in closed beta five years ago, we bet everything on the browser. Like many others that used Google Docs at school and then returned home to virtual worlds, we intuitively understood that Internet native software embodies values like collaboration, transparency, and access. Pretty much everyone around us—friends, classmates, coworkers we had interned with—shared these values, so we assumed they were self-evident.
>
> We didn't realize that launching Figma was heresy, a generational assault on top-down, siloed models of decision-making and a challenge to the identity of many designers.

He continued:

> Now I understand that the power of the browser lies in the broader cultural change it delivers—and this change can be scary. The browser is natively multiplayer. It forces a mindset shift on access. It strips away

> the need for expensive hardware. And it pushes us to embrace working together, especially when we are blocked and our default might be to hide.[43]

Fortunately, Field and Wallace were unbowed. Fans of the platform's intuitive, easy-to-use interface quickly outnumbered detractors. Figma continued adding capabilities, including 2019's Figma Community, enabling users to share design kits, systems, and files; and 2021's FigJam, a whiteboarding tool that allows both designers and nondesigners to brainstorm ideas. In 2022, Google for Education and Figma partnered to bring the platform to education Chromebooks free of charge. Field said, "We actually built Figma with Chromebooks in mind from the start. Back in 2015–2016 we were testing our tools with Chromebooks."[44] In 2023, in response to user research indicating that developers weren't as happy working in Figma as designers, Figma launched Dev Mode, which streamlines the handoff from design to development and fully welcomes developers into the fold.

In the meantime, Adobe took note. While Adobe's creative suite—which includes well-established products like Photoshop, Illustrator, Acrobat, After Effects, and more—still dominated as design tools, Figma suddenly controlled the workflow space Adobe's tools populated. Still, when Adobe announced its intention to acquire Figma (retaining Field as CEO, "running the business with autonomy")[45] for the spectacular sum of USD 20 billion, there was a great deal of public head-scratching. Why such a sum for a company that had never been valued at anything close?

In the *Guardian*, technology professor and author John Naughton cited two key reasons. First, quoting analyst Ben Thompson, "Figma is set to be the 'operating system for design,' which means that in the long run Adobe has to operate on Figma's terms, not the other way around." Second, in Naughton's own words, "The other reason is that Figma was doing quite nicely and had no need to sell itself. So the offer had to be one that nobody could refuse."[46]

Whatever the thinking behind the merger, Figma and Adobe went into the planned partnership in good faith and with grand visions for what the partnership could achieve. Regulators, however, feared that the merger would reduce competition in a market Adobe already dominates. Margrethe Vestager, the head of the European Commission's competition policy, said in a statement, "It is important in digital markets, as well as in more traditional industries, to not only look at current overlaps but to also protect future competition."[47]

The would-be partners read the room and parted ways, with Adobe paying Figma the billion-dollar reverse termination fee. As Yahoo! Finance assessed in March 2024, "Empowered by a substantial cash infusion, Figma wasted no time charting its course forward." In the wake of the failed merger, Figma projected USD 600 million in annual recurring revenue for 2023 (a 50 percent increase from 2022) and moved to acquire Dynaboard, a real-time, multiplayer web app design platform.[48]

Figma built its success by understanding what users needed from workflows. Its product, competitive, and growth strategies—initially born of instinct, "youthful confidence," and a sense of play—were refined by understanding what users wanted that competitors *weren't* providing. Further, by agreeing to a win-win merger with its biggest competitor, it was ultimately left stronger standing on its own: regulators and the market have firmly stated that Figma has its own role to play in the future of design.

Mind the Risk Exposure Gap—and the Risk Opportunity Gap

These companies' divergent experiences over the same time period vividly illustrate that it is not the risk conditions themselves that ultimately determine whether value is created or destroyed. The deciding factor is how companies manage these risk conditions.

Succeeding in permacrisis demands a risk management solution that can better respond to growing risk velocity and volatility. Otherwise, the speed of risk and value destruction will continue to widen the risk exposure gap I mentioned at the beginning of the book, in which risk demands far exceed most organizations' capacity to address them.

I see a flip side to the risk exposure gap, however: an "opportunity exposure gap." After all, if we don't have adequate resources in the three lines, we will not only be more vulnerable to risks—we may also be more oblivious to opportunities.

Figma is the last featured case study for a reason. The thinking that engendered the company's collaborative design platform is also the thinking we need for effective risk management in the modern age. As CEO Field wrote in 2020:

> One of the best parts of my job as CEO of Figma is playing anthropologist. Over the past five years, I've seen firsthand how working in a collaborative digital space moves teams from a mindset of "my ideas" to "our ideas." This requires a radical shift—a level of trust and transparency that many of us are still catching up to.[49]

Before exploring the "radical shift" needed for risk management, however, we must take a deeper dive on the current risk landscape and its impact on organizations. We need to understand why and how the resulting challenges have resulted in an unsustainable state of affairs—the risk exposure gap—that leaves organizations vulnerable.

Part 2

The Widening Risk Exposure Gap

CHAPTER 4

The Daunting Risk Landscape

We've set the scene: the risk landscape is forever changed, as one disruptive risk event after another asserts its profound interconnectedness and inability to be contained. The first half of the 2020s has given the business schools of the future an abundance of case studies in risk-induced value destruction and creation. Permacrisis demands risk management transformation at every level of the organization.

These unprecedented conditions have yielded a growing risk exposure gap—the widening gulf between the risks an organization faces and its capacity to manage those risks. The risk exposure gap modern organizations face is created by two principal factors: the rapid expansion of critical risks and the limited (and largely stagnant) pool of resources organizations have to assess and address these risks. Bridging the gap is absolutely vital for operational resilience and enabling organizations to achieve their strategic objectives.

In this section, we take a closer look at the current risk landscape to gain a clearer picture of the risks facing organizations today. Then, we explore the roots and ramifications of the resource limitations confronting organizations. Lastly, we examine the myriad problems manifesting in organizations due to the risk exposure gap.

In chapter 2, "Emergence of Permacrisis," we looked at the extraordinary sequence of risk-related events that have dominated the past five years, but there are yet more risks at work. Armed with the hindsight we've gained from the first half of the 2020s, let's examine today's dominant risks through a more strategic lens to include insight and foresight.

Today's Top Global Risks

I often give the advice to "follow the risks." Of course, risk in permacrisis is a continually moving target. Understanding the need for risk management transformation necessitates bringing into clearer focus the chief risks facing today's organizations. To gain an appropriately broad perspective, I draw from a range of externally produced surveys, reports, and analyses, many of which are updated annually. As business leaders and boards strive to understand the risks impacting their business, these external resources offer highly valuable perspectives grounded in data that look toward the future. The primary resources referenced include:

- The World Economic Forum's (WEF's) *Global Risks Report*, which draws its findings from global leaders across business, government, academia, civil society, and the international community
- *Executive Perspectives on Top Risks*, a collaboration between Protiviti and NC State University's ERM Initiative focused on capturing insights from C-suite executives and directors
- The *Global Technology Audit Risks Survey*, a survey conducted by Protiviti and The IIA that assesses risks across all three lines as well as through the lenses of IT audit leaders and CAEs
- The Internal Audit Foundation's (IAF's) *Risk in Focus—North America* and *North America Pulse of Internal Audit* and AuditBoard's *Focus on the Future Report*, surveys that focus on capturing internal audit leaders' perspectives
- KPMG's *Chief Ethics & Compliance Officer Survey* and *Chief Risk Officer Survey*, which hone in on insights from CCOs and CROs, respectively
- EY's *Global Board Risk Survey*, which gathers insights on top risks as seen by boards
- The *Audit Committee Practices Report* from the Center for Audit Quality and the Deloitte Center for Board Effectiveness, which delivers the audit committee perspective

Digital Risk

Technology has become essential to delivering value and meeting stakeholder expectations. Accordingly, the ability to leverage technology to drive innovation, efficiency, productivity, and competitive differentiation has become a strategic objective for most organizations. But as technology continues its relentless advance, governance and risk management have not kept pace. Digital risk—the risk manifested by the creation, delivery, and use of technology processes, products, and services in business operations—ranks among the most pervasive, fast-growing, and potentially impactful risks facing any organization. Digital risk expands exponentially as organizations race to capitalize on emerging technologies.

Digital transformation without effective governance and risk management creates an astounding range of new vulnerabilities that can lead to unwanted business outcomes. From externally originating threats such as data breaches, ransom demands, and third-party security failures to internal problems such as fraud, data manipulation, and system malfunctions, these highly disruptive incidents can wreak operational, financial, and reputational havoc that destroys value at a truly tectonic level. Data breaches in particular can yield astronomical costs: IBM's *Cost of a Data Breach Report 2024* records an all-time high average total cost of a data breach at USD 4.88 million.[1]

Next, we'll hone in on some of the most significant technology-related risks.

Cybersecurity

Cybersecurity continues to be a top risk area for organizations globally. *Executive Perspectives on Top Risks* assesses, "Cybersecurity is the most pressing risk when combining near- and long-term views," citing "growing recognition of a complex cyber risk landscape that is impacted by the exponential curve of technological advances, increasing reliance on third parties, and other market forces."[2] The *Global Technology Audit Risks Survey* finds that more than 75 percent of respondents across all three lines consider cybersecurity to be a high-risk area.[3] Drilling down to second- and third-line perspectives only elevates the perceived threat levels:

- Within the *Global Technology Audit Risks Survey*'s overall group of respondents, 82 percent of CAEs and IT audit directors rank cybersecurity as a high-risk threat.[4]
- Risk executives surveyed in KPMG's *2023 Chief Risk Officer Survey* rank cybersecurity threats as the #2 challenge facing their organizations within the next two to five years.[5]

While cybersecurity has ranked at or near the top of all risk categories facing organizations globally for more than a decade, too many organizations continue to express surprise when they fall victim to a cyberattack. Business leaders and boards must move forward with a clear-eyed view on not only the realities of cybersecurity risk, but the effectiveness of their organizations' cyber risk management. No organization can afford an attitude of overconfidence.

The SEC's cybersecurity rules, which took effect in September 2023, put significant regulatory weight behind this reality. The mandate requires public companies to formally disclose material cybersecurity incidents to the SEC within four business days. To ensure the speed and accuracy required for identifying these incidents, assessing their materiality, and reporting them in such a tight time frame, organizations must continuously monitor for cyber incidents and materiality.

Leaders at private companies may assume this legislation does not impact them. That's not the case. The SEC cybersecurity rules are indicative of other cybersecurity legislation on the horizon, much of which extends its scope beyond public companies. Furthermore, private companies are often third parties to public companies—and thus potentially liable for any cyber incidents impacting their public company partners. At any rate, cybercriminals do not discriminate: in proposing its new rule, the SEC cited a 2023 study showing that 98 percent of organizations use at least one third-party vendor that experienced a breach in the past two years.[6]

Emerging Technologies

Emerging technologies hold amazing promise as well as ample risk. Organizational use of generative AI, blockchain, the Internet of Things, robotic process automation (RPA), quantum computing, and other emerging technologies create fundamental challenges in terms of integration with legacy systems, cybersecurity threats, ethical considerations, and other essential questions. Indeed, business leaders see plenty worth worrying about: *Executive Perspectives on Top Risks* ranks "rapid speed of disruptive innovations enabled by new and emerging technologies and/or other market forces" as the fourth-ranked risk for 2034.[7]

Artificial Intelligence

AI in particular presents threats and opportunities on a scale witnessed few times in history. Beyond raising ethical considerations around bias, discrimination, fraud, and lack of accountability or transparency, AI presents serious questions around hallucinations, accuracy, accountability, data privacy, intellectual property, legality, regulation, compliance, workforce disruption, and job displacement. WEF's *Global Risks Report* cites "adverse outcomes of AI technologies" as the sixth-ranked global risk on the 10-year horizon.[8]

Further, as organizations race to capitalize on AI's potential, governance is not keeping pace. A 2023 ISACA poll of more than 2,300 audit, risk, security, data privacy, and IT governance professionals finds:

- Only 28 percent of surveyed organizations expressly permit generative AI use.
- Most organizations' employees are nonetheless using generative AI: 41 percent say their employees are using it—and another 35 percent aren't sure.
- Only 10 percent say their organizations have a formal, comprehensive policy for generative AI.
- More than 25 percent say that they have neither a policy nor plans to create one.
- Fewer than one-third, however, say that AI risk is an immediate priority.[9]

AI will have a far more enduring effect on our world than anything else that has happened over the course of the past five years. While other events will continue to be disruptive, their impact will pass. During a recent meeting with AI experts, I heard one make the observation that he thought AI would be "as fundamentally transformational to human civilization as electricity." I wholeheartedly agree and will continue exploring AI's potential and impact throughout this book.

Misinformation and Disinformation

Misinformation (false or inaccurate information) and disinformation (false or inaccurate information that is deliberately intended to mislead) are on the rise on social media platforms and the Internet in general. WEF's *Global Risks*

Report views misinformation and disinformation as a critical accelerating risk, ranking it #1 among all risks on the two-year horizon.[10] *Executive Perspectives on Top Risks* also spotlights these risks, calling out the potential impact to how organizations do business, interact with customers, ensure regulatory compliance, and protect their brands.[11]

Of course, misinformation and disinformation risk impacts societies worldwide, helping to escalate polarization, exacerbate other social and political divides, impact elections, undermine governments, and promote unrest, further increasing geopolitical instability. The threats presented by misinformation and disinformation will only grow as AI tools that can generate and spread it become more sophisticated and widely available.

Data Privacy

Data privacy continues to be a massive risk for every organization, whatever their business model and wherever they operate. *Executive Perspectives on Top Risks* ranks it tenth overall for 2024.[12]

Data privacy is also among the most perplexing risks to navigate, given the deeply complex and growing web of data protection regulations and compliance obligations covering the globe. The EU's General Data Protection Regulation (GDPR), first adopted in the EU in 2016, has rapidly gained traction on a global basis. United Nations data indicates that 78 percent of countries worldwide have passed data protection and privacy legislation, and an additional 4 percent of countries are currently in the process of drafting legislation.[13] According to the tracker maintained by the International Association of Privacy Professionals, 19 U.S. states have enacted comprehensive data privacy laws, and more states are likely to follow.[14] These laws are having a massive impact. In 2023, Meta was fined a record USD 1.3 billion for violating EU rules by transferring data to the U.S. from EU Facebook users.[15]

As stated in *Privacy and Data Protection*, a 2024 report from Crowe and the IAF, "One noteworthy trend in the evolution of the regulatory environment is a growing consensus that recognizes privacy as a fundamental human right."[16] Organizations cannot afford to be careless in this area, and those with risk exposures in multiple jurisdictions must pay special attention.

Limitations of Legacy IT Infrastructure

Executive Perspectives on Top Risks ranks "existing operations and legacy IT infrastructure unable to meet performance expectations as well as 'born digital' competitors" as a top-10 risk concern for both 2024 (seventh-ranked) and 2034 (eighth-ranked).[17] Business leaders seem increasingly cognizant that their aging IT infrastructure can have far-reaching impacts not only on the quality, cost, profitability, time to market, and ongoing innovation of their products and services, but also on their ability to adapt to change, integrate with advanced technologies, detect risks and issues (including those that may trigger cybersecurity and data privacy concerns or exposures), and effectively manage their third-party risks and relationships.

It's not only the "born digital" competitors that executives should worry about. As the report calls out, other competitors may be "investing heavily to leverage technology for competitive advantage."[18] We'll take a detailed look at how technology can both help and hinder organizations in chapter 11.

Macroeconomic Conditions

Globally and in the U.S., widespread macroeconomic woes continue to plague both organizations and the societies in which they operate.

- *Executive Perspectives on Top Risks* ranks "economic conditions, including inflationary pressures" as its top risk for 2024 and seventh-ranked risk for 2034, and "change in current interest rate environment" as its eighth-ranked risk for 2024.[19]
- The WEF's *Global Risks Report* counts lack of economic opportunity, inflation, and economic downturn as its sixth-, seventh-, and ninth-ranked risks in the next two years.[20]
- From a second- and third-line perspective, 33 percent of risk executives in the *2023 Chief Risk Officer Survey* identify "economic downturn or recession" as a top-five risk facing their organizations in the next two to five years[21], and 41 percent of internal audit leaders surveyed in *2024 Risk in Focus—North America* rank "market changes" as a top-five risk.[22]

Although a "softer landing" appears to be prevailing, inflationary pressures, the current interest rate environment, rising tariffs and border restrictions, an ongoing cost-of-living crisis impacting low- and middle-income households, supply-side price pressures, and a general sense of economic unease and uncertainty will continue to impact operations, costs, and margins and restrict opportunities for growth.

The reality is that many audit, risk, compliance, and InfoSec professionals had never actually experienced inflation firsthand before this decade. As a young internal auditor starting out in the latter half of the 1970s, I didn't know any other environment than one in which inflation presented ongoing risks for my organization. Until the 2020s, however, inflation hasn't been the norm for more than 40 years, and guidance isn't easy to find.

Organizations should understand that they are likely to face challenges in effectively budgeting and forecasting; managing surging costs and other expenses, including talent, infrastructure, raw materials, and capital; and effectively adjusting prices to maintain margins. They should also be mindful of the second- and third-order risks inflation may pose, including fraud, capital market volatility, and supply chain disruption.

Globalization and Geopolitical Instability

Events in one part of the world can create ripple effects everywhere else. The Peterson Institute for International Economics defines globalization as "the growing interdependence of the world's economies, cultures, and populations, brought about by cross-border trade in goods and services, technology, and flows of investment, people, and information."[23]

Thus far, the 2020s have been a profound lesson in the far-reaching impacts of globalization. Ambiguity, uncertainty, and instability seem to be the only identifiable constants. In the preface to the *2024 Global Risks Report*, WEF Managing Director Saadia Zahidi paints a dire picture of a world beleaguered by conflict, worry, and frustration.

> Underlying geopolitical tensions combined with the eruption of active hostilities in multiple regions is contributing to an unstable global order characterized by polarizing narratives, eroding trust and insecurity. At the same time, countries are grappling with the impacts of record-breaking extreme weather, as climate-change adaptation efforts and resources fall short of the type, scale and intensity of climate-related events already taking place. Cost-of-living pressures continue to bite, amidst persistently elevated inflation and interest rates and continued economic uncertainty in much of the world. Despondent headlines are

borderless, shared regularly and widely, and a sense of frustration at the status quo is increasingly palpable.[24]

Risks have become interrelated on a global scale, and the first half of the 2020s has been characterized by a truly startling number of world-altering events. COVID-19 highlighted pandemics' potential for widespread disruption, as well as the anxious longing for normalcy we would all feel in its wake. Geopolitical tension is widespread, with remarkable geopolitical shifts seemingly underway in many regions. As an unthinkable war in Europe wore on, an unspeakable war in the Middle East followed on its heels. Unstable government regimes, shifting political climates, growing polarization, and terrorism continue to be abundant worldwide. Natural disasters and climate change continue to exacerbate both physical and supply chain risks.

These forces and countless others contribute to an overall risk climate of uncertainty and ambiguity. With all these conflicts happening amidst a seemingly constant state of change, boards and executives are rightly asking, "What's next?"

The risks of geopolitical instability and globalization should be an important element in many organizations' risk portfolios, monitored as a component of effective risk management. Regrettably, they are rarely given the level of attention they warrant—until it's too late, and organizations are caught by surprise by unexpectedly brutal downstream impacts. In my experience, risk and assurance professionals do not often focus on the risks of globalization and political instability. Even though board members surveyed in EY's *Global Board Risk Survey 2023* rank "geopolitical events (e.g., increasing nationalism, trade wars)" as the top source of risk likely to have a severe impact on the organization during the next 12 months, a relatively low number (43 percent) count geopolitical risk as part of their governance oversight.[25]

Third-Party Risk

Gone are the days when an organization's suppliers or partners were entirely well-known and highly trusted third parties. In the interconnected global economy of the 2020s, your organization is likely purchasing raw materials, goods, and services from business entities halfway around the world. In turn, these third parties work with their own third parties, creating a labyrinthine Nth-party web extending far beyond your organization's knowledge or control.

Your organization can be impacted by anything that happens in that far-flung ecosystem. In particular, third- and Nth-parties' financial stability, carbon footprint, data security weaknesses, intellectual property, AI usage, working conditions, and hiring practices can all have a distinct impact on yours.

This is why third-party risk is a rapidly expanding risk universe unto itself, encompassing wide-ranging categories such as financial, operational, strategic, reputational, ESG, digital, geopolitical, regulatory/compliance, fraud, corruption, cybersecurity, data privacy, supply chain, business continuity and resiliency, and beyond. *Executive Perspectives on Top Risks* ranks third-party risks as the fourth-ranked risk for 2024 and sixth-ranked risk for 2034.[26]

The trend of organizations relying on third parties for critical business processes accelerated during the COVID-19 pandemic. Organizations are often outsourcing key functions and relying on business partners and IT vendors for others. While increasing reliance on third parties can absolutely yield monumental benefits, organizations navigating the risk climate of the 2020s should be particularly mindful of the following third-party risks:

- **Data privacy and security.** Third parties and third-party technologies often have access to sensitive company data. A third-party data breach can expose your organization to financial, legal, and reputational costs.
- **Business continuity and resiliency.** Service outages or failures at third parties relied on for core business functions can challenge organizations' operations, performance, reputation, customer and business relationships, and capacity to pivot.
- **Regulatory compliance.** In some regulatory areas, organizations may be held liable for noncompliance from third or even Nth parties in their supply chains, resulting in legal issues or lofty fines.

Regulatory Changes and Scrutiny

I've written in the past that the arc of the regulatory pendulum tends to swing wider in times of crisis. This is certainly bearing out amid permacrisis. The pace of regulatory change continues to accelerate, adding layer upon layer of complexity to an already intricate web of compliance obligations and placing fresh demands on organizations to modify their processes, products, services, and policies to enable compliance. There has been a notable uptick in regulatory scrutiny in key areas, including data privacy; ESG, an area in which integrated reporting requirements are proliferating both globally and in the U.S.; and cybersecurity, given the new SEC requirements mandating public company reporting of material cybersecurity events. Potential laws to regulate social media and AI are also looming.

C-suite leaders don't expect this pressure to let up within the next 10 years: respondents in *Executive Perspectives on Top Risks* rank "heightened regulatory changes and scrutiny" as the fifth-ranked risk for both 2024 and 2034. While the survey calls out specific requirements worrying the financial services and technology sectors, it adds:

> Such concerns are pervasive across other industries, as worries about expanding government regulations and agency enforcement—particularly related to data privacy, climate disclosures, sustainability reporting, cyber breach disclosures, expanded attestation requirements, and other matters—are higher than reported in last year's survey for both the coming year and a decade out.[27]

Second- and third-line perspectives reinforce the pervasiveness of these worries.

- Risk leaders in KPMG's *2023 Chief Risk Officer Survey* rank regulatory changes and compliance issues as the top challenge facing their organizations in the next two to five years.[28]
- In *2024 Risk in Focus—North America*, 43 percent of internal audit leaders rank regulatory change as a top-five risk facing their organization, making it the third-ranked risk overall.[29]
- KPMG's 2024 *Global Chief Ethics and Compliance Officer Survey* finds that 84 percent of CCOs expect regulatory expectations and scrutiny to continue rising over the next two years.[30]

Overall, the wave of new laws and regulations—both those that have already crashed against the shore and those expected to crest in the near future—is further contributing to organizations' uncertainty about the future.

Sustainability

Organizations face an ever-widening range of sustainability risks. There are the obvious near-term physical risks caused by sudden and severe weather events (e.g., wildfires, hurricanes, floods), which can damage facilities and infrastructure and disrupt supply chains. There are also physical risks brought on by the short- and long-term impacts of resource scarcity and rising temperatures and sea levels. Organizations should be especially mindful of evolving stakeholder expectations around sustainability, increasing the potential for reputational impacts and noncompliance with regulations.

Globally, interest in sustainability and other ESG-related issues has escalated dramatically since 2020. With climate change, COVID-19, and social change movements as a backdrop, investors, governments, regulators, consumers, employees, and other stakeholders have been examining and recalibrating their expectations for how businesses can be held accountable for responsible ESG performance. Investors in particular want to know how sustainability-related risks impact your organization and its current and longer-term financial performance and position. They want to make the most informed decisions they can, and regulators worldwide are heeding their call.

At the regulatory level, this has resulted in no less than a global transformation in the sustainability risk disclosure landscape. The past few years have witnessed the simultaneous implementation of all of the following:

- The EU's Corporate Sustainability Reporting Directive (CSRD) and associated European Sustainability Reporting Standards (ESRS)
- The UK's Climate-related Financial Disclosure Regulations
- The inaugural S1 and S2 standards issued by the IFRS Foundation's International Sustainability Standards Board (ISSB)
- The SEC's final rules for the Enhancement and Standardization of Climate-Related Disclosures

Even though these regulations typically phase in compliance over time, no organization should put off taking action to put in place the necessary processes, controls, and technologies to support accurate, complete, reliable, and audit-ready reporting on climate-related risk.

Rising Talent Shortages and Labor Costs

The talent market continues to tighten and evolve, making it increasingly difficult for organizations to navigate the changing expectations of talent, generational differences, succession challenges, and rising compensation demands. Respondents in *Executive Perspectives on Top Risks* rank the "ability to attract, develop and retain top talent, manage shifts in labor expectations, and address succession challenges" as the #2 risk overall both globally and in North America.[31] Talent risk is also high on board members' radar, with 42 percent of respondents in EY's *Global Board Risk Survey 2023* assessing that "people issues, such as talent shortages or the failure to upskill" are likely to have a severe impact on their organizations in the next year.[32]

Competition for talent is fierce across all three lines. Organizations are finding it increasingly difficult not only to find resources with the specialized skills they seek, but also to find resources, period. Inflationary pressures are further complicating the picture: respondents in *Executive Perspectives on Top Risks* cite the tightening race for talent as likely to drive increasing labor costs both now and well into the future.[33]

Organizational Culture

Culture is one of the most substantial yet overlooked risks in any organization, as an organization's culture impacts nearly every aspect of risk management. Culture is also a key factor in enabling successful transformation in any area of the business.

Professionals across the three lines are starting to better understand culture's contributions to organizational success. Unfortunately, this growing awareness doesn't always translate to action. Culture risk actually fell in many surveys' rankings. Yet, the risk is real, and board members seem to agree: 42 percent of the respondents in EY's *Global Board Risk Survey 2023* judge that "misaligned culture" is a source of risk likely to severely impact their organizations within the next year.[34]

In such a tight talent market, organizations should not underestimate culture's enormous impact on attracting and retaining talent.

- The *2022 EY US Generation Survey* found that 92 percent of workers say company culture has an impact on their intent to stay with their current employer.[35]
- Respondents in a Gallup survey who feel strongly connected to their culture indicate they are 55 percent less likely to look for another job, four times more likely to be engaged at work, and five times as likely to recommend their organization as a great place to work.[36]

A Perfect Storm of Risks—and Limited Risk Resources

The risks examined here represent only some of the dominant risks we already know about. Organizations must also ask themselves: What downstream impacts will these risks create? What new risks will emerge seemingly out of nowhere? Perhaps most critically, will they have the resources they need to meet these growing risk demands?

It is particularly important to understand risks and impacts in the context of each risk area's threat level relative to the organization's level of preparedness. That's precisely why the question of resource and skill shortages in key risk areas should loom large for every organization. As such, this is the very question our next chapter addresses.

CHAPTER 5

Stagnant Resources

The argument thus far seems clear enough: with risk mounting and permacrisis promising a state of persistent crisis, the way we manage risk must evolve. Risk resources across all three lines—those who daily bring their skills, knowledge, experience, and decisions to bear to identify, assess, mitigate, monitor, and provide assurance regarding risk—remain the vital core of any effective risk management program. With new risks emerging with ever greater velocity and volatility, demand is rising for risk resources with the right expertise to help organizations address all of the key risks they face, plus the myriad unknown risks waiting beyond the horizon.

Unfortunately, the resource pool is stagnant at best. There are dire shortages of in-demand skill sets in critical technology areas (e.g., cybersecurity, AI, cloud computing, managing adoption of digital technologies), as well as in key second- and third-line functions. There are simply not enough resources to go around for many roles. What's more, employee expectations and preferences are shifting, reflecting priorities beyond the old standbys of salary, benefits, and stability—and the growing impact of AI and automation will further change the game.

Against this formidable backdrop, every organization strives to build the next-generation team they need to help them navigate the demands and risks they'll face in the future. But as we've seen, most are challenged to find sufficient capable resources to meet current needs.

This is a true talent crisis. While the word "crisis" is often overused or misused, it is the most accurate term in this context, given the complex and massive challenges it creates for organizations. Resource stagnation severely limits our ability to not only keep step with risks but also evolve, innovate, and strategically position our organizations for relevance, resilience, and future success. In fact, "stagnation" may be an understatement when describing the situation in many organizations where audit, risk, and compliance resources are in genuine decline.

Talent management risk is here to stay, which means board members and business leaders ignore it at their considerable peril. In this chapter, we'll look at the factors and forces limiting the flow, growth, and development of the resources organizations need to reduce the risk exposure gap.

The Evolving Ecosystem of Talent Risk

As outlined in the previous chapter, attracting, retaining, and developing talent has become a top concern for boards and business leaders in nearly every sector and geography. They increasingly understand how talent risk limits their ability to achieve their objectives or meet stakeholder expectations.

Talent's interconnectedness with other risks is also becoming more evident. For example, third-party and digital risks swell exponentially as organizations rely on more third parties to support core business operations. Operational, financial, and reputational risks compound alongside capacity shortfalls, high turnover, deflated morale, troubled cultures, and rising recruitment, development, and labor costs. Competitive differentiation and advantage are also at stake, as organizations fail to gain access to the specialized skill sets and fresh perspectives essential to innovation. I could go on and on. Instead, let's hear from the boards and business leaders themselves about talent's interconnection with other key risks.

Intensifying Third-Party Risk

We've taken a detailed look at how boards, C-suite leaders, and second- and third-line functions are prioritizing third-party risk. That said, its escalating priority level is worth a second look relative to the "war for talent."

Among all 36 of the most top-of-mind risks highlighted in *Executive Perspectives on Top Risks*, third-party risk's ranking increased the most of any risk from the prior-year report, moving from 17th position in 2023 to fourth position in 2024. Third-party risk also ranks in executives' forward-looking top-10 list for 2034, coming in at sixth position.[1]

The report ultimately suggests a direct link between the remarkable increase in rank and executives' heightened focus on "new risks that may emerge in light of these external partnerships." These risks arise from many organizations' increased use of joint ventures, alliances, and other third-party relationships to fill the gaps created by talent management challenges.[2] In other words, as our talent management challenges increase, so (likely) does our third-party risk.

Growing Skill Shortages in Key Areas

Technology

Organizations' ability to understand and manage technology-related risk—as well as their ability to leverage technology to gain a competitive edge—depends on their ability to access high-quality technology talent. But as McKinsey's *Technology Trends Outlook 2023* warned, "There's a wide gap between the demand for people with the skills needed to capture value from the tech trends and available talent: our survey of 3.5 million job postings in these tech trends found that many of the skills in greatest demand have less than half as many qualified practitioners per posting as the global average." In particular, McKinsey's report tracks significant growth in job postings around applied AI, next-generation software development, cloud and edge computing, trust architectures and digital identity, and the future of mobility.[3]

Many organizations are already feeling the impact of this gap. According to the 2024 *Global Technology Audit Risks Survey* from Protiviti and The IIA, nearly half of the organizations surveyed see significant gaps between the skills available in their organization and the skills needed for effective risk management and technology adoption. Approximately 44 percent of respondents cite "lack of technical skills" as a top-three barrier to adopting IT audit tools and technologies, and 45 percent of respondents believe that their technology audit department needs enhanced training to more effectively manage both current and emerging technology risks, making it the top-ranked response overall.[4]

The cybersecurity profession in particular is facing an increasingly dire shortage. Findings from the ISC2 2023 *Cybersecurity Workforce Study*, which surveyed nearly 15,000 cybersecurity practitioners and leaders globally, help illustrate the prodigious size of the gap and the problem it creates.

- In 2023, roughly four million cybersecurity professionals were needed worldwide. To be at full capacity, the profession needs to almost double.
- More than two-thirds of respondents (67 percent) report having shortages of cybersecurity staff needed to prevent and troubleshoot issues, and 92 percent report having skills gaps.
- Three out of four respondents view the current threat landscape as the most challenging it has been in the past five years, and a little more than half (52 percent) believe their organization has the tools and people needed to respond to cyber incidents over the next two to three years.[5]

Risk Management, Internal Audit, and Compliance

Organizations simultaneously face a shortage of next-generation talent in risk management, internal audit, and compliance. The impact of this shortage is increasingly top-of-mind for many audit committee members: when asked to rank their top priorities for the next year, audit committee members surveyed in the 2024 *Audit Committee Practices Report* select "finance and internal audit talent" as their #3 priority, coming after only cybersecurity (#1) and ERM (#2).[6] While I regret the survey's need to lump finance and internal audit into a single category, that is nonetheless some very impressive company.

The roots of this growing shortage extend in many directions:

- Workforces are aging and retiring. For example, *Strategic Risk* reports that 68 percent of risk managers in the U.S. are over the age of 40, and only 6 percent are between the ages of 20 and 30.[7] A U.S. Senate report on *America's Aging Workforce: Opportunities and Challenges* finds that the number of older workers in the U.S. is growing at a rate outpacing the overall growth of the labor force: whereas the entire labor force is projected to grow by an average of only 0.6 percent between 2016 and 2026, the number of workers aged 65 to 74 is projected to grow by 4.2 percent annually and the number of workers aged 75+ by 6.7 percent annually.[8]
- Fewer people are entering these fields. Many of these areas have historically relied on accounting students to help fill their ranks, but they are now drawing from a shrinking pool of applicants. The AICPA's *2023 Trends Report* finds that bachelor's degree completions in accounting dropped 7.8 percent in 2021–2022 from

prior-year figures—and this drop comes on the heels of a steady decline of 1–3 percent since the 2015–2016 academic year.[9]

- Perceptions of these professions are suffering. Some young professionals perceive a lack of opportunities for career development and upward mobility. Others simply have an erroneous view of the work, viewing it as dull, repetitive, or lacking in worthwhile challenges. Still others worry that these roles are likely to be replaced by automation and AI in the not-too-distant future. This last concern is a valid worry; we'll examine this question more fully as we proceed.
- Many people are simply quitting. As a 2023 *Wall Street Journal* article reports, those already in the profession—suffering from heavier workloads and less support—are often opting to "jump ship." Data from the Bureau of Labor Statistics' 2023 population survey indicate that more than 300,000 accountants quit their jobs between 2019 and 2021.[10] Further, as the *Wall Street Journal* reports in another article, other data shows that a rising percentage of accountants are leaving their careers in later years: employment data provider Live Data Technologies finds that approximately 82 percent of accountants who left the profession from January 1 to September 1, 2023, had at least six years of experience.[11]
- Employees lack critical skills needed for the future. The *RIMS Risk Management Talent 2025 Report*, for example, finds that nearly all respondents (94 percent) believe that risk management professionals need new skills to meet future challenges—and only 32 percent of executive leaders believe that today's risk management professionals are prepared.[12] Protiviti's 2023 *Next-Generation Internal Audit Survey* assesses that fewer than 6 in 10 internal audit functions have access to the talent they need across next-generation competencies such as continuous monitoring, high-impact reporting, dynamic risk assessments, agile auditing, advanced analytics, automation, process mining, ML, AI, strategic vision, and talent management.[13]

The shrinking of traditional talent pools for risk management, internal audit, and compliance, alongside the widening skills gap, demands that organizations reimagine their approach to recruiting and retention. I have been waving this flag for years, encouraging audit, risk, and compliance functions to look to nontraditional sources for talent, explore ways to make day-to-day work more meaningful, engaging, and motivating, and invest in employee development that better fits the preferences of the next generation.

Shifting Employee Expectations

Changing employee expectations are absolutely impacting the problem of stagnating resources. Beyond clear differences in generational preferences around jobs and workplaces, the COVID-19 pandemic altered how many of us think about our work.

I will always look back on 2020 as a life-changing year. For the previous 11 years, I'd been the CEO of a global organization and a globe-trotting spokesman for internal audit. Suddenly I was a homebound executive, and the forced experiment enabled me to peek into an alternative version of my world. The experience likely accelerated my decision to pass the torch to a new CEO in early 2021.

My experience was not unusual. The Great Resignation saw a significant number of U.S. employees voluntarily leaving their jobs, citing low pay, poor work-life balance, lack of benefits or advancement opportunities, or feeling generally unappreciated in their workplaces. As the Great Resignation seemed to be on the wane, the Quiet Quitting phenomenon, in which deeply unengaged employees report doing the bare minimum to meet their responsibilities, began gaining attention in its stead. While analyses of both phenomena have been somewhat overblown in the media, organizations should gain a better understanding of the different generational priorities expressed.

A deep analysis of these differences is beyond the scope of this book, but the overall message is increasingly cogent: Different generations of workers have different priorities, preferences, goals, and day-to-day needs. Any organization that intends to attract, retain, and meaningfully develop these workers must be mindful of these changing preferences. These considerations should inform not only talent management strategy, but also organizational structure, leadership and communication styles, physical environment, policies (e.g., flexibility, remote work, compensation, recognition, benefits, incentives, code of conduct), mission and value statements, strategies for building and maintaining a healthy culture, and even technology selection.

The Accelerating Impact of AI and Automation

Automation and AI capabilities are also impacting the talent crisis. This impact will only escalate in the years to come.

Certainly, organizations benefit from realizing efficiencies that enable them to deploy bandwidth and talent elsewhere. The WEF's *Future of Jobs Report 2023* suggests that the impact of most technologies on jobs is expected to be a net positive over the next five years.[14] A 2023 ISACA poll of audit, risk, security, data privacy, and IT governance professionals relates that 85 percent of respondents view AI as a tool that extends human productivity, and 62 percent believe it will have a positive or neutral impact on society as a whole. Their outlook, however, is not entirely rosy: 45 percent believe that a significant number of jobs will be eliminated due to AI, and 80 percent believe they will need additional training to keep their jobs or move forward in their careers.[15]

A *Newsweek* story on the jobs most at risk of being replaced by AI mentions many of the jobs that might readily spring to mind, given AI's burgeoning capabilities in consuming, analyzing, and synthesizing large amounts of data. These jobs include data analysts, bookkeepers, customer service representatives, media content creators, legal assistants and paralegals, and financial analysts.[16]

A 2023 Accenture report judges that banking could be hardest-hit by AI deployment, assessing that up to 54 percent of the sector's tasks could be automated by generative AI. Insurance, software/platforms, capital markets, energy, and communications/media are the next most impacted sectors. The report further suggests that 40 percent of working hours across industries can be impacted by large language models (LLMs).[17]

No role is exempt from the growing impact of AI and automation. The 2023 *edX AI Survey* asked 800 C-suite executives about various aspects of AI's impact.

- A resounding 77 percent say AI is disrupting their business strategy, and 79 percent fear that an inability to learn how to use AI will leave them unprepared for the future of work.
- They collectively estimate that more than half (56 percent) of entry-level roles will be eliminated.

- Nearly half (47 percent) believe that most or all of the CEO role should be completely automated or replaced by AI—and 49 percent of the CEOs in the group agree.[18]

According to a *New York Times* article, some organizations are already experimenting with AI CEOs. Anant Agarwal, the founder of edX and a former director of MIT's Computer Science and AI Lab, estimates that 80 percent of the work a CEO does can be replaced by AI. Agarwal also believes that AI will help to democratize top management roles: "There used to be a curve of people who were good with numerical skills and those who were not. Then the calculator came along and was the great equalizer. I believe AI will do the same thing for literacy. Everybody could be CEO."[19]

The overarching reality is that organizations are likely to struggle to take a human-centric approach to adopting AI and automation. This not only increases the potential for displacement in both blue- and white-collar jobs, but puts traditional talent management methods, organizational culture, and governance under renewed pressure.

Skills Mismatch Requires a Fundamental Shift

The stagnation of the risk resource pool, happening in tandem with the technological advances of AI, automation, machine learning, data analytics, and other emerging technologies, is presenting organizations and human workers alike with new and profound challenges. In particular, it's becoming clear that there will be a fundamental shift in how we understand and value different skill sets. The WEF's *Future of Jobs Report 2023* indicates that approximately 44 percent of workers' skills will be disrupted in the next five years.

> Cognitive skills are reported to be growing in importance most quickly, reflecting the increasing importance of complex problem-solving in the workplace. Surveyed businesses report creative thinking to be growing in importance slightly more rapidly than analytical thinking. Technology literacy is the third-fastest growing core skill. Self-efficacy skills rank above working with others, in the rate of increase in importance of skills reported by businesses. The socio-emotional attitudes which businesses

> consider to be growing in importance most quickly are curiosity and lifelong learning; resilience, flexibility and agility; and motivation and self-awareness. Systems thinking, AI and big data, talent management, and service orientation and customer service complete the top 10 growing skills. While respondents judged no skills to be in net decline, sizable minorities of companies judge reading, writing and mathematics; global citizenship; sensory-processing abilities; and manual dexterity, endurance and precision to be of declining importance for their workers.[20]

The report includes a fascinating and multifaceted look at the skills rising and declining in importance. Figure 5-1 includes the top 10 skills identified.

Figure 5-1
Top 10 Skills on the Rise

Share of organizations surveyed that consider skills to be increasing or decreasing in importance, ordered by the net difference.

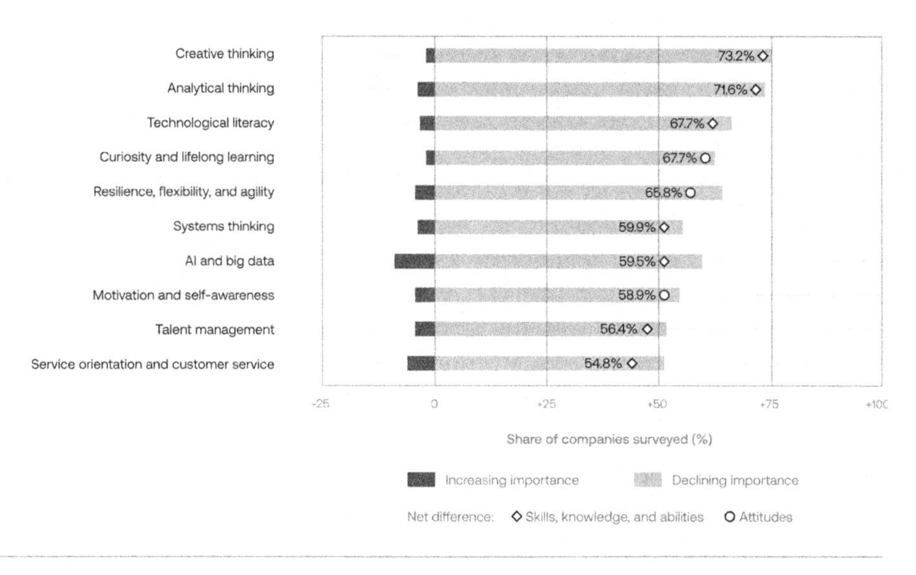

Source: World Economic Forum, Future of Jobs Survey 2023.

All this to say, some skills will be devalued as others increase in importance. How will organizations evolve their talent management strategies to source or cultivate these skills? How will human workers adapt in the face of this fundamental shift?

Human workers already say they feel increasingly replaceable. The University of Phoenix's *2024 Career Optimism Index* finds that more than half (53 percent) of Americans say that they are "easily replaceable in their job position."[21]

We will have to fundamentally alter our thinking about how we—as human beings—continue to add value that consistently exceeds the capabilities of generative AI. Humans ultimately need to move toward roles that AI can't easily replicate, such as those requiring emotional intelligence, creativity, complex problem-solving skills, and nuanced judgment. Organizations need to invest in rethinking roles, and in retraining and reskilling programs to help employees transition to these roles.

The big picture is still coming into view, but it's already clear that AI's potential impact on the workforce poses key risks to organizations and is likely to further inflame the talent crisis.

Risk Demands and Capacity Shortages Collide

As we've shown, even though risks are more voluminous, diverse, and uncertain than ever, organizations are typically not deploying additional audit, risk management, compliance, and InfoSec resources to address these risks. Rather, they're facing a stagnant resource pool severely lacking in qualified professionals with the specialized skills needed to manage many of today's most pressing risks. Further compounding the problem, they often lack comprehensive talent management strategies.

What's more, even if organizations were able to fully staff their teams, they would still struggle in the face of mounting risk and uncertainty. Rising risk demands are colliding with an ongoing talent crisis, manifesting in insufficient capacity and capability to address risk. The outcome is an unsustainable risk exposure gap, and it should be every organization's top priority to address it. Figure 5-2 depicts how rising risk volume meets resource limitations to create the gap.

Figure 5-2
The Risk Exposure Gap

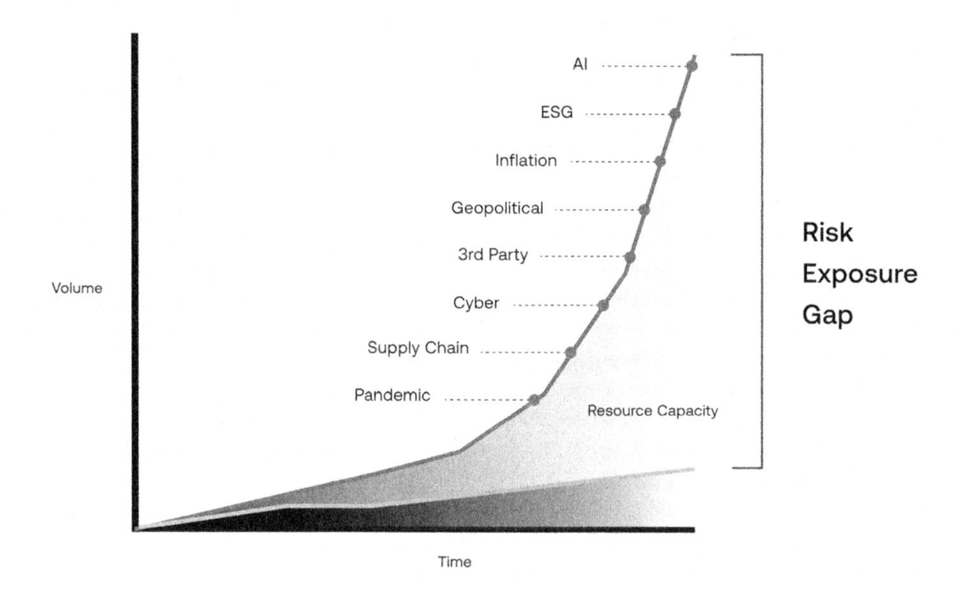

Now that we have a better understanding of the forces that are creating the risk exposure gap, we can take a closer look at how the gap impacts organizations in the short and long term. What problems does it create and why? How do these problems put value creation at risk?

CHAPTER 6

The Unsustainable Risk Exposure Gap

The risk exposure gap prevents organizations from managing risk effectively, pursuing value creation opportunities, and achieving their strategic objectives. Bridging the gap is vital for both protecting and creating value for stakeholders, and for creating organizations that are agile and operationally resilient. Resilient organizations are able to withstand impacts, adapt and respond accordingly, and navigate successfully amid changing circumstances.

What impact is the risk exposure gap having on your organization? Where and how is it most likely to manifest? While the gap can reveal itself in countless ways, we'll explore several of the most common symptoms in this chapter.

As your organization strives to become more strategic, proactive, and forward-looking in its approach to risk management, it's imperative to take an honest and comprehensive look at the impact current practices are having on your operations, decision-making, performance, strategy, talent management, resiliency, reputation, potential for noncompliance, and beyond.

What the Gap Looks Like

The risk exposure gap is dynamic and multidimensional; the degree to which it manifests in organizations, as well as the specific indicators signaling its presence, will vary. The following symptoms are nonetheless exceedingly common in many organizations.

Legacy Tools/Approaches and Low Technology Adoption

Operations frequently rely on labor-intensive, error-prone manual processes, disjointed tools and technologies, disconnected processes, and fragmented, outdated data to manage risk. Teams are making do with bolt-on technologies that don't work together or share data, further hardening silos and creating obstacles to collaboration. Technologies being used may cause friction with inferior user experiences that aren't purpose-built or integrated into workflows. Further, because there is no unified data core, AI tools can only be deployed with limited effectiveness.

C-suite executives and directors seem well aware of the limitations and vulnerabilities created by legacy IT systems, including those used by audit, risk, and compliance professionals: as mentioned in chapter 4, respondents in *Executive Perspectives on Top Risks* ranked "existing operations and legacy IT infrastructure unable to meet performance expectations as well as 'born digital' competitors" a top-10 risk for both 2024 and 2034.[1]

Siloed Teams

First-line management and audit, risk, compliance, and InfoSec teams tend to operate independently of one another and have not established formal avenues of communication and collaboration. These teams often speak different languages, rely on inconsistent definitions and taxonomies, and deliver perspectives that are out of alignment with one another to management and the board. Generally speaking, they are also not capitalizing on opportunities to learn from each other's perspectives and (where appropriate) rely on each other's work. Surveys often reveal only informal or inconsistent communication and collaboration between audit, risk, and compliance teams, with no formal strategy connecting their efforts. For example, in describing current levels of interaction between ERM and internal audit, respondents in AuditBoard's *2024 Focus on the Future Report* survey—an effort I lead annually—report that only 9 percent of functions coordinate on all major aspects of managing enterprise risks.[2]

I have begun thinking of this persistent siloing in even less flattering terms: teams are too often retreating into their proverbial "caves" to undertake their mission. In the sanctity of their caves, others can't interrupt, complicate, or interfere with their work. They may genuinely feel they do their best work this way, but operating in isolation undoubtedly slows communication, hinders resource sharing, reduces coordination, and impedes productivity and efficiency.

Lack of First-Line Engagement and Ownership

First-line teams play a pivotal role in detecting and mitigating risks and implementing policies and processes. But clunky technology—paired with poor user experience and a lack of integration with day-to-day workflows—often means that first-line owners aren't meaningfully engaging with audit, risk, and compliance technologies. Failing to see a direct connection to and value for their work or roles, they're less likely to engage in risk management or recognize their capacity to do so.

Lack of Continuous Monitoring

Organizations lack the ability for true continuous monitoring of risks and controls, sufficing with risk assessments performed annually or quarterly. That's not continuous, and that's not what's needed. Risk assessments are only point-in-time snapshots; without real-time tracking of key risk indicators (KRIs) and other internal and external risk indicators, companies are left vulnerable. You may see CAEs or risk leaders consulting with business and functional management and other risk functions—a practice that can be a powerful tool within a larger continuous monitoring scheme. However, continuous monitoring approaches based largely on the ideas and opinions of others don't go far enough. We will return to this topic in chapter 13.

Ongoing Talent Management Challenges

Job applicants may turn down roles—or existing employees may leave their positions—after assessing that the organization isn't prioritizing technology investments. The brightest professionals seek opportunities to learn valuable skills that will help them advance their careers. This typically includes the opportunity to use next-generation technologies. Young professionals in particular are likely to see overreliance on outdated, clunky legacy technology as a foreboding and unattractive red flag.

How the Gap Impacts Organizations

Boards and business leaders across all three lines are well-served to gain a more precise understanding of how much is at stake for organizations that do not take action to address the risk exposure gap. In situations where leadership has pushed back on transformation efforts focused on risk management and technology, spotlighting the consequences outlined in this section may prove useful.

Lost Productivity and Limited Efficiency

It's not rocket science to understand that manual processes, operating in tandem with disconnected data and tools, make audit, risk, compliance, and InfoSec work and reporting more labor-intensive, time-consuming, error-prone, and low-value. With so much time and effort spent on traditional work and administrative duties, critical risk resources have precious little capacity to focus on more strategic or higher-value activities. Their highly valuable, increasingly limited time—time which could undoubtedly be better spent driving impact—is lost and devalued. Also likely to be lost are top talent, who will quickly become frustrated and dissatisfied working in such an environment.

Duplication of Effort and Audit Fatigue

Risk teams' focus areas inevitably overlap and intersect, so without deliberate coordination, their work (e.g., data gathering/aggregating, controls testing, risk assessments) is often redundant. Efforts to respond to risks may be similarly duplicative, with teams pursuing their own disaggregated solutions. Plus, control owners often receive duplicative information requests, leading to audit fatigue. These repeated requests for input on risk assessments or documentation/evidence are often inconsistent and cumbersome. Nobody appreciates having to provide the same information to different requesters multiple times throughout the year.

Further, duplication of effort and audit fatigue are significant contributors to the soaring costs of second- and third-line functions. Audit, risk, compliance, and InfoSec teams are often asking for more resources, with budgets increasing accordingly. Will first-line leaders, executive management, or board members see value in having members of several different teams ask them the same questions? Or worse yet, how will they respond when these teams parade in front of them with different perspectives and solutions on key risks facing the organization?

Gaps in Risk Coverage

Inefficient processes, paired with the lack of concerted coordination and information-sharing between audit, risk, compliance, and information security teams, can also create significant coverage gaps, opening up new risks and vulnerabilities. With nobody responsible for reviewing the full body of these teams' work, how can organizations ensure that all key risks are receiving appropriate focus?

They largely can't. Like ships passing in the night, each team goes about their work largely unaware of other teams' work and perspectives—such that each may assume others are addressing some key aspect of risk management, when in fact nobody is. Without deliberate back-and-forth communication, it's impossible to know what the other teams are thinking or doing, what risks they're identifying and prioritizing, and how they assess the organization's overall risk management. In these types of environments, identifying and closing gaps generally happens retroactively. This often means that a coverage gap has already invited an unwanted outcome that negatively impacted the organization.

This is not a state of affairs that any organization should willingly embrace as the expected way of tackling risk management. Sadly, it remains the status quo in many organizations.

As mentioned, most organizations' legacy technologies and processes lack the ability to continuously monitor risks, leaving organizations struggling to identify, assess, and mitigate key risks, effectively monitor KRIs, meet regulatory requirements, or track efforts to improve operations and performance. While we'll explore continuous risk monitoring strategies in detail in chapter 13, the important thing to understand at this juncture is that a lack of continuous monitoring capabilities—paired with the inability to identify risks in real time—means that risks and issues are much more likely to fall through the cracks.

This scenario opens the door to potentially existential threats to the enterprise. To survive permacrisis, organizations must build in the capacity to identify and monitor the seeds and early warning signs of developing crises. Equally important is for an organization's risk resources to enable the organization to find any available silver linings among the clouds crowding the horizon, so that crisis can be turned into opportunity when possible.

Poor Data Quality and Availability

Today's organizations create more data than ever. With so many different pools of data in so many different hands, it's incredibly challenging to ensure that risk data remains up to date, reliable, and readily available to the stakeholders who need access to it. Given heightened customer expectations and regulatory burdens (e.g., cybersecurity, ESG, data privacy), this lack of data quality and availability also increases reputational risk, compliance risk, and others.

Further, data controls are often inadequate, leaving organizations with a poor understanding of who is accessing and updating what data and when. Most organizations also lack visibility into how risk data is being collected, stored, protected, and shared within and beyond the organization, further increasing their data privacy, cybersecurity, and third-party risk.

Fast-Increasing Digital Risk

As we addressed in chapter 4, too many organizations are investing in digital solutions without making the investments needed to govern and connect them. As single-purpose solutions proliferate across audit, risk, and compliance, so do the costs to maintain them. Plus, as technology use increases across the organization—often occurring as "shadow IT" or "shadow AI," unknown to, and unregulated by, the organization's central IT function—so do the digital risks its use creates. This elevates the risk of unwanted business outcomes such as unauthorized access, data breaches or leakages, identity theft, errors, system malfunctions, erroneous IT administration, fraud, ransom demands, third-party security failure, data manipulation, deletion, vandalism, or other cybercrimes.

The truth is that most organizations don't actually know what's in the software they're using, and thus fail to understand their risk and take timely action to find and patch vulnerabilities. That's exactly why many of the vulnerabilities exploited by cyberattackers will continue to plague organizations for years to come. For example, the U.S. Government's Cyber Safety Review Board estimates that the highly damaging Log4Shell/Log4j vulnerability will continue to affect systems until at least 2032.[3]

A 2022 report from the Consortium for Information & Software Quality estimates that the cost of poor software quality in the U.S. has ballooned to at least USD 2.4 trillion, and that the accumulated software technical debt has now reached USD 1.52 trillion.[4] Make sure your organization's share of these costs is not unnecessarily large.

Lack of Connection Across Risk Data

Without a unified data core that constitutes a single source of truth, data integrity is regularly called into question and reporting becomes distinctly less valuable to decision-makers. Risk data is obviously crucial information to get right because it typically includes business strategies and objectives, enterprise risks, individual risk statements, KRIs, issue data, company policies and procedures, control frameworks, internal control objectives and testing procedures, testing and assurance work, compliance requirements, and more. Are you willing to ask management to base critical decisions on risk prioritization and mitigation on conflicting sets of largely unverified data?

Lack of Risk Visibility and Context

Disconnected data and processes and audit, risk, compliance, and InfoSec teams retreating into their caves results in a lack of visibility into—and a deficient understanding of the context surrounding—other teams' risk data, insights, and priorities. These teams frequently miss out on vital opportunities to use each other's insights and work to inform their audit planning, risk assessments, and prioritization.

With inadequate context around the various teams' data and insights (including their assessments of the highest-risk areas), the organization is left with a woefully incomplete view of its risk and threat landscape. This significantly reduces management's and the board's ability to understand the relationships between risks or to understand where efforts should be invested to deliver the most value. For example, how is the team charged with managing ERM to correctly assess enterprise risks without easy access to residual risk information from other teams or clear visibility into the assurance work being performed?

Lack of Real-Time Risk Identification or Insight

In the face of the risk exposure gap, organizations don't have the data or insights they need to enable fast, timely responses to emerging risks or make more risk-informed decisions. Without real-time access to (and visibility into) the full scope of the organization's risk data, teams cannot quickly identify emerging or changing risks or surface actionable risk insights. This weakens first-line teams' ability to quickly respond to emerging risks, and audit, risk, compliance, and InfoSec teams' capacity to serve as trusted partners to the business. Instead, the organization becomes mired in simply reacting to risks and issues.

As teams proceed along separate paths—often manually tracking issue and action plans and embarking upon separate solutions to the same or related problems—their ability to have an impact or reach swift resolution is lessened. While no silver bullet exists for identifying emerging risks, permacrisis demands we do better.

Lack of Alignment or Common Language

Many audit, risk, compliance, InfoSec, and even first-line teams speak different languages when they talk about risk. They may use different risk and process definitions, rating systems to quantify risks (e.g., color coding; stoplights; high, medium, low), methodologies, and KRIs. Different groups' risk assessments often consider disparate attributes to quantify risk, making it difficult to meaningfully compare assessment results.

This lack of alignment can lead to many undesirable outcomes. Audit plans may not keep pace with the organization's changing business needs and risk profile. Teams are unable to leverage effectively—let alone rely on—other teams' work. What's more, when audit, risk, compliance, and InfoSec teams aren't even aligned with one another, how can the organization ensure they're aligned with its priorities, strategies, and stakeholder expectations, and not operating with discordant goals?

The most unfortunate outcome of this lack of alignment for many organizations, however, is that management and the board regularly receive different perspectives from different advisors. Decentralized data and disaggregated reporting (e.g., findings, issues, perspectives, priorities) make these teams' communications to boards and executives difficult to understand and potentially conflicting. How can management make decisions effectively, or boards provide effective oversight, when they're receiving inconsistent or even incompatible viewpoints?

I've heard this feedback ad infinitum from executives and boards who receive completely different perspectives on risk from internal audit, risk, compliance, InfoSec, and external audit. Their confusion compounds when nobody is using the same lenses, data, terminology, or rating systems. As one exasperated audit committee chair told me, "We tell them to go away and have a conversation, and come back when they can speak the same language. And if they still disagree, tell us why."

Lack of Resilience

Any combination of the earlier impacts easily reduces organizational resilience. *PwC's Global Crisis and Resilience Survey 2023* defines resilience in three dimensions:

1. **Strategic resilience,** or the ability to evolve and build agility into the organization
2. **Operational resilience,** or the ability to maintain critical operations during disruption
3. **Financial resilience,** or the ability to maintain capital and cash flow during disruption[5]

Improving resilience should be a vital strategic objective for every organization. Doing so requires committing to improve how data, insights, perspectives, and work are shared among all the key risk teams. As Peter Bäckman's 2022 LinkedIn article observed, modern ERM requires resilient organizations to shift from the reactive to the proactive and consciously cultivate a risk-aware culture across the organization.[6]

As the WEF and McKinsey report *Building a Resilient Tomorrow: Concrete Actions for Global Leaders* writes, "Leaders need to move toward putting resilience into action." To that end, they suggest:

- Developing a new resilience leadership mindset
- Creating a resilience agenda that addresses short- and long-term risks and opportunities
- Assessing the organization against a resilience framework
- Developing methodologies to factor resilience into decision-making
- Measuring and communicating resilience status to stakeholders

- Developing financing and insurance mechanisms to de-risk resilience
- Setting up public-private partnerships to promote collaboration[7]

A Mandate for Transformation

Ultimately, the multilayered impacts created by the risk exposure gap put organizations' ability to achieve their strategic objectives—including value protection, realization, and creation—in considerable peril. They also make it incredibly difficult for audit, risk, compliance, and information security team members to become the trusted advisors their organizations urgently need during times of permacrisis.

As I shared in the previous chapter, the WEF's *Future of Jobs Report 2023* finds that organizations now consider "resilience, flexibility, and agility" a top-three core skill for their workforce, only ranking lower than "analytical thinking" and "creative thinking."[8] Indeed, the leading organizations of the future will take this priority to heart, understanding that in our treacherous risk climate, an inability to adapt leads only to obsolescence.

Complacency is not a strategy. Our growing crisis and urgent imperative is to improve collaboration across traditional lines using a connected risk approach. Visionary leaders spanning the three lines must take action now to communicate this urgency and help architect a better path forward. Before diving into the specifics of the solution, however, let's take a closer look at why the old model isn't working—and how we can begin reimagining it to enhance risk management and solve for the risk exposure gap.

Part 3

Siloed Risk Management Creates Its Own Risks

CHAPTER 7

Risk Management Is the Means, Not the End

Why isn't effective collaboration already happening across the three lines? One key piece of the puzzle is that some organizations' key risk players make the mistake of treating risk management as an end in itself. Another piece stems from the history of risk management.

First, consider the industry and business model where risk management first originated. As former COSO Chairman Paul Sobel explained:

> "Internal audit as a profession has a pretty long history. Risk management, a little less so. But the roots came out of the insurance industry, and insurance itself is an end product. You hope something doesn't happen—but if it does, the insurance company will step in and at least reduce the impact. So in many companies, that more strategic risk management mindset is still taking hold."

Further, as noted in chapter 1, it took time for risk management to gain traction—but soon enough, it gained sufficient credibility that many people began to think of risk management itself as the be-all and end-all. By viewing the vital activities of risk management as their mission-critical goal, I believe these professionals lost focus on the outcome of effective risk management: supporting organizations in achieving their objectives.

Unfortunately, by focusing on "what" we do versus "why" we do it, we overlook what is most important: whether our work contributes to results that are aligned with the organization's ability to create value.

This chapter looks at how different risk teams' focus on their individual activities and purposes has not only exacerbated the problem, but also created hurdles that organizations must overcome on the path to transforming risk management.

Valuing Individual Activities over Organizational Results

Each key player in risk management has a unique purpose to fulfill. For some teams, however, these purposes become conflated with the specific activities for which they are responsible. Indeed, as we become immersed in our own team's fundamental activities, it's not hard to lose focus on the bigger picture surrounding them.

It's also understandable that risk and assurance teams take pride in having high-quality processes. We are passionate about our work, gravitating toward roles that offer day-to-day work we enjoy. The problem emerges when we begin to value the processes themselves over the value they are intended to deliver and the ends they are designed to serve.

As a young internal auditor, I took the quality of my workpapers very seriously. I was painstaking in documenting the results of my work, believing that well-organized, comprehensive workpapers were critical to demonstrating the quality of my efforts. Indeed, workpapers are critical in providing the basis for audit reports. But the problem emerged when—bowing to the prevailing thinking at that time—I began believing that the more workpapers I created, the better. I truly thought that documenting my evidence in such scrupulous detail demonstrated the value of my internal audit engagement.

After I became a CAE, my perspective changed quickly and dramatically. I realized that my team's enthusiasm for documentation was translating not only to a shocking amount of paper, but also to a great deal of time misspent. The process was inefficient, time-consuming, and low-value, usurping our capacity to take on higher-value activities that contributed actual value for the organization.

Workpapers are important. But workpapers are only the means by which the audit results are documented, and overly detailed workpapers slow down the internal audit engagement and ultimately do a disservice to the organization.

Each of the three lines has its own equivalent examples of my "workpapers." These activities and processes enable us to showcase our passion, strengths, and acumen. However, they are not the reason we manage risks. They are only valuable insofar as they drive the desired results and enable our organizations to achieve their objectives.

As the executive summary to COSO's 2017 ERM framework states, "Enterprise risk management is not a checklist."[1] It is not a set of tasks to be done, an inventory, or a specific function or department. Risk management doesn't exist for the sake of managing risk. It runs to a larger, overarching purpose and universal objective for all organizations: preserving, creating, and sustaining value for stakeholders.

Different Purposes with a Shared Goal

Audit, risk, compliance, and InfoSec teams contribute to effective risk management in different ways, serving distinct but equally valid and respected purposes. It is simultaneously undeniable, however, that they share a common goal—contributing to the success of the organizations they serve. After all, how can any of them claim success if the organizations they jointly serve fail? This mutual mission is where they can and should align.

The reality, however, is that how these teams view their roles and missions has created and hardened silos that often prevent them from communicating and collaborating effectively. The following pages offer a closer look at these key players' roles relative to risk management, detailing both individual purposes and how they align with the organization's objectives.

Historically, these teams have often concentrated on their individual roles over the common threads that should unite them. If they focus more consistently on the ways their purposes overlap, informing and supporting one another, they improve the likelihood of engendering meaningful, productive communication and collaboration.

Risk Management

Individual purpose:

- Identify, assess, monitor, and communicate risk to help first-line teams better anticipate, manage, and mitigate threats and capitalize on value-creation opportunities.
- Consider risk relative to internal controls, strategy, governance, performance measurement, compliance requirements, and stakeholder expectations and communications.
- Support the organization in embedding risk management in its governance, structure, processes, policies, objectives, strategy, decision-making, values, and culture.

Organizational alignment:

As described by COSO and ISO:

- Enable the organization to manage and mitigate risks that could impact its ability to achieve its objectives.
- Avoid surprises while increasing the likelihood of positive outcomes.
- Enhance governance, performance, and resilience; improve decision-making and resource deployment.
- Enrich management dialogue by adding perspective (based on changing conditions) on the strengths/weaknesses of the organization's strategy.

Internal Audit

Individual purpose:

- Assess risk to build and maintain dynamic risk-based audit plans.
- Bring objectivity and a disciplined, systematic approach to evaluate and improve the effectiveness of risk management, governance, and controls.
- Provide independent assurance that risk management, governance, and controls are adequate and operating effectively.

Organizational alignment:

As described in The IIA's Standards, enhance the organization's:

- Successful achievement of its objectives
- Governance, risk management, and control processes
- Decision-making and oversight
- Reputation and credibility with its stakeholders
- Ability to serve the public interest[2]

Compliance

Individual purpose:

- Assess risk to identify and communicate the organization's most critical compliance risks, determining what obligations apply.
- Ensure the organization is operating ethically and in accordance with applicable laws and regulations.
- Set standards and provide guidance and training to enable the organization to implement the standards effectively.

Organizational alignment:

- Support the organization in building, strengthening, and preserving a culture of compliance and ethics that helps prevent problems before they begin.
- Safeguard the organization's reputation, the trust of its stakeholders, and its ability to deliver value to those stakeholders.
- Enable the organization to abide by and promote compliance and ethical standards to contribute to the public interest.

InfoSec

Individual purpose:

- Assess risk to identify IT-related risks and protect the organization's IT systems, infrastructure, and data from threats, theft, and vulnerabilities.
- Help develop and implement controls and processes to mitigate IT risks, including those needed to support compliance with laws/regulations relative to data privacy, cybersecurity, and other IT-related areas.
- Maintain an optimal IT security posture.

Organizational alignment:

- Enhance organizational resilience by identifying and mitigating issues before they disrupt operations or cause losses (e.g., financial or reputational damage).
- Ensure ongoing data quality, confidentiality, integrity, and availability.
- Enable the organization to make risk-informed decisions about how and where to invest resources for cyber and other technology controls.

Once again, note the commonality across all of these functions' purposes: to ensure organizations achieve their objectives, including protecting, creating, and sustaining value. That is the thread running through the entire risk management community—the shared objective around which all parties can coalesce.

This overarching objective also illustrates why greater communication, collaboration, and alignment are needed. A connected risk approach is a natural way for teams to come together to make it happen.

Understanding the Hurdles to Collaboration

Successfully implementing connected risk requires first overcoming the significant hurdles to collaboration that have historically persisted in many organizations. Management and boards—as well as audit, risk, compliance, and InfoSec practitioners themselves—should strive to understand these obstacles. In this way, they become better equipped to reduce concerns and encourage appropriate methods for overcoming them.

Several of these hurdles originate from viewing risk management as the product rather than the process. We contribute to the problem when we:

- Use risk management activities as opportunities to showcase the quality of our skills or get credit for our achievements.
- Value our own comfort and preferences over what's best for our organizations.
- View technology selection and implementation through a function-specific lens.
- Allow concerns about independence to prevent internal audit from providing first- and second-line teams with guidance on designing and implementing risk management.

These are all natural and understandable tendencies. However, they do not contribute to effective risk management. Let's make sure we understand why.

Proving Value and Wanting Credit

It's only human to want to prove one's worth through individual achievements. This message is powerfully reinforced by what we hear from our parents, how we are graded in schools, and how most employers recognize and reward performance. Proving value or aptitude in these contexts most often emphasizes individual performance. Is it any surprise that so many professionals emerge with an ingrained attitude of "This is my job and I can do it myself"?

Certainly, we all enjoy getting credit for a job well done. We feel proud to be singled out when we have worked hard or gone the extra mile. We can't help the nagging feeling that proving one's value is more easily done by working independently.

This attitude, however, is not conducive to effective risk management in today's organizations. Chapter 6 examined the many drawbacks that a lack of communication and coordination can create. The growing risk exposure gap insists that we do better—and recognizing that we need to check our egos and desire for credit at the door is a solid first step. Sobel captured this sentiment well.

> There's very much a human factor at work. I don't think enough people within organizations have the right level of humility to recognize they can't do it all on their own. It sounds like such common sense. But we really have to approach it as, "I don't care whether it's your idea or my idea. As long as it's good for the company, then it's a good idea. Let's do it." The matter of who takes credit is not that critical.

This tendency to want credit is compounded by the fact that, historically, risk and assurance professionals' performance was often measured based on individual outputs, such that a bigger-picture focus on the outcomes those outputs supported was occasionally lost. For example, though the risk register was a valuable evolution in how internal audit approached its work, establishing the foundations for the now well-established practice of risk-based auditing, auditors must learn to look beyond it as they strive to showcase their value. As Sobel expressed, "It's not about the risk register, the risk universe, or even the risk assessment. It's ultimately about understanding uncertainty well enough that management can figure out how to make better decisions."

In chapter 10, we'll invest more time in understanding how the historical focus on outputs over outcomes may be holding us back. For our current purposes, suffice to say that each of us must acknowledge if and how the desire for individual credit is impeding us from offering more to our teams.

Resistance to Change

Also at work is a simple reluctance to embrace change. It's human nature to want to do things as one has always done them, taking confidence and comfort in the processes and technologies with which one is already familiar. Nevertheless, to avoid future obsolescence, every profession must evolve alongside the tools, technology, body of knowledge, and conditions in which it operates.

Many years ago, I coined the term "Jurassic Auditors" to describe internal auditors who tended to cling to outdated practices. I used the term because the incredible majority of species from the Jurassic period became extinct due to a failure to adapt. I reintroduce it here as a warning to any "Jurassic" audit, risk, compliance, and InfoSec professionals still dwelling on the past. As John F. Kennedy said, "Change is the law of life. And those who look only to the past or the present are certain to miss the future."

Silos Hardened by Legacy Technologies

As audit, risk, compliance, and InfoSec teams' scopes and mandates have grown and changed over the past several decades, they have increasingly looked to technology for support. Early on, the demand created the supply: technology companies readily answered the call, building solutions custom-fit to each team's unique needs and priorities. Every function seemingly had its favorite technology; over time, the popularity of single-purpose solutions ballooned and the capacity for customization increased.

Organizations often let individual functions select and implement their own technologies. Early on, there was little sense of needing a "grand plan," because the technology landscape was changing so quickly. The thinking was that each team knew its own needs best, and these single-purpose solutions were the best these teams could hope for at the time. Of course, technology companies diligently worked to improve them, adding features and functionality in their quest to dominate their chosen markets.

Many teams still use these single-purpose legacy technologies. Unfortunately, these technologies typically are not designed to support cross-functional collaboration, data sharing, or reporting. Accordingly, as individual functions became more reliant on their own tailored technology solutions that did not integrate well with one another, they also became more siloed.

Internal Audit Concerns about Independence

Another part of the problem is that many risk and assurance professionals have been conditioned to stay in their metaphorical caves to establish and retain credibility. Internal auditors in particular may feel the need to seek protection from allegations of a lack of independence or objectivity. This often creates an ingrained reluctance to collaborate. This reluctance can run rather deep. Recently, as I was preparing for a risk management industry seminar focused on driving alignment across the three lines, I was cautioned, “You have to be careful not to use the word collaboration.” The gist of their message was that many audit and risk practitioners don’t believe “collaboration” is a word that should *ever* be used in connection with the profession.

I wish this were surprising, but I’ve long known that the “collaboration” terminology is problematic for some. I’ve spoken with countless internal auditors over the decades who greatly resist the term, viewing it as contradictory to or compromising their independence.

I have long been an advocate for greater collaboration across the three lines, and I see independence concerns as navigable. It’s important to remain respectful, however, in discussing these concerns. Independence has long been a part of internal audit’s core identity, so some hesitation about collaboration is understandable. I find it helpful to focus the discussion on the differences between independence and objectivity, and on appropriately defining how independence is achieved. The following pages offer guidance in both areas.

Overcoming the Hurdles to Collaboration

Distinguishing between Independence and Objectivity

Objectivity and independence are not the same thing.

The concept of independence is an organizational attribute. That is, internal audit is organized independently within the enterprise, enabling it to fulfill its mandate of objectivity. As we'll explore later in this chapter, internal auditors must confirm their independence to the board at least annually, communicating any potential impairments. Further, **Standard 6.2 Organizational Independence** states that the internal audit charter must include the "reporting relationships and organizational positioning of the internal audit function, as determined by the board," documenting how internal audit's independence is supported.[3]

That said, no internal audit function is without a degree of "dependence" on the organization for which it provides assurance. Be they contractors or employees, internal auditors are part of—and dependent for their paychecks upon—the organizations they serve. This dependence, however, does not preclude internal audit from remaining objective, and objectivity is central to internal auditors' concerns relative to preserving their independence.

As I wrote in my book *Agents of Change: Internal Auditors in the Era of Permacrisis*:

> Objectivity is an unbiased mental attitude that allows internal auditors to go into an engagement with no preconceived notion of what they are going to find and perform their work without compromise...Objectivity is critically important in that it promotes internal audit as a true broker of assurance. When internal audit reports on the health or wellness of a control or process, its objectivity is at the heart of its credibility.[4]

From my experience, objectivity impairments are more likely to undermine internal audit's effectiveness than its independence. Collaborating with risk managers and compliance professionals benefits the enterprise. If we take the lead in fostering greater collaboration, our independence is not compromised.

Fortunately, objectivity is a state of mind. As professionals in control of their own states of mind, internal auditors can collaborate without yielding their objectivity.

Collaborating does not require relinquishing control of one's objectivity. No strong, independent-minded internal auditor would allow their objectivity to be eroded simply because they have collaborated on something that provided overall benefit to their organization.

Relying on Professional Standards and Guidance

Fortunately, professional standards and guidance from The IIA can also help us lower some of the perceived hurdles to collaboration.

The IIA's 2020 Three Lines Model

Let's begin by looking at what The IIA's Three Lines Model says relative to internal audit independence. As I've often affirmed—and as The IIA's 2020 update of the model explicitly stated—"independence does not imply isolation."

The IIA's 2020 position paper further stated (emphasis added):

> There **must be regular interaction between internal audit and management** to ensure the work of internal audit is relevant and aligned with the strategic and operational needs of the organization. Through all of its activities, internal audit builds its knowledge and understanding of the organization, which contributes to the assurance and advice it delivers as a trusted advisor and strategic partner. **There is a need for collaboration and communication across both the first and second line roles of management and internal audit to ensure there is no unnecessary duplication, overlap, or gaps.**[5]

The update also specifically addressed how internal audit independence is achieved. **Principle 5: Third-line independence** stated:

> Internal audit's independence from the responsibilities of management is critical to its objectivity, authority, and credibility. It is established through: accountability to the governing body; unfettered access to people, resources, and data needed to complete its work; and freedom from bias or interference in the planning and delivery of audit services.[6]

The IIA's 2024 *Global Internal Audit Standards*

The IIA's professional standards for the practice of internal audit also specifically address questions of independence, objectivity, and collaboration.

The *Standards* have long addressed the perceived conflict of operationally working for management while serving the organization's overall interests. However, the new *Standards* released in 2024 further strengthen the well-established distinction between independence and objectivity.

Standard 7.1 Organizational Independence establishes and affirms internal audit's independence from management. It also provides CAEs with the confidence and ability to review (and even potentially criticize) management without fear of reprisal.[7]

Further, the new standards don't simply *allow* internal audit to collaborate with the first and second lines. They explicitly encourage it. As I reviewed **Standard 9.5 Coordination and Reliance** in detail, I began thinking of it as the "connected risk standard," given the many parallels of the standard's language with the more collaborative risk management approach I am recommending.

The "Requirements" section of 9.5 provides the directive while highlighting the benefits (emphasis added):

> The chief audit executive *must coordinate with internal and external providers of assurance services and consider relying upon their work.* Coordination of services minimizes duplication of efforts, highlights gaps in coverage of key risks, and enhances the overall value added by providers.
>
> If unable to achieve an appropriate level of coordination, the chief audit executive *must raise any concerns with senior management and, if necessary, the board.*[8]

Notably, The IIA uses the safer term "coordination" in this section. But 9.5's "Considerations for Implementation" section provides a list of "examples of coordination" that could just as accurately be labeled "examples of collaboration."

- Synchronizing the nature, extent, and timing of planned work

- Establishing a common understanding of assurance techniques, methods, and terminology
- Providing access to one another's work programs and reports
- Using management's risk management information to provide joint risk assessments
- Creating a shared risk register or list of risks
- Combining results for joint reporting

9.5's "Considerations for Implementation" further states (emphasis added):

> The chief audit executive considers the organization's confidentiality requirements before meeting with the various providers to gather the information necessary to coordinate services. Frequently, the **providers share the objectives, scope, and timing of upcoming engagements and the results of prior engagements**. The providers also **discuss the potential for relying on one another's work**.

It also says (emphasis added):

> The chief audit executive **may choose to rely on the work of other providers** for various reasons, such as to assess specialty areas outside the internal audit function's expertise, to decrease the amount of testing needed to complete an engagement, and to **enhance risk coverage beyond the resources of the internal audit function**.[9]

Additional standards reflect this increased emphasis on coordination and collaboration—several of which don't shy away from using the term "collaboration."

Standard 9.3 Methodologies "Considerations for Implementation" states that documented methodologies necessary to implement internal audit's strategy and plan and conform with *Standards* include the internal audit function's approach to "coordinating with internal and external assurance providers."[10]

Standard 11.1 Building Relationships and Communicating with Stakeholders "Requirements" stipulate that (emphasis added):

> Chief audit executives **must develop an approach for the internal audit function to build relationships and trust with key stakeholders,**

including the board, senior management, operational management, regulators, and internal and external assurance providers and other consultants. The chief audit executive **must promote formal and informal communication between the internal audit function and stakeholders**, contributing to the mutual understanding of:

- Organizational interests and concerns
- Approaches for identifying and managing risks and providing assurance
- Roles and responsibilities of relevant parties and **opportunities for collaboration**[11]

Standard 10.3 Technological Resources "Considerations for Implementation" recommends that—"to evaluate whether the internal audit function has technological resources to perform its responsibilities"—the CAE should "collaborate with other departments on shared governance, risk, and control management systems."[12]

Standard 3.1 Competency "Considerations for Implementation" suggests that internal auditors should develop competencies related to "communication and collaboration."[13]

In summary, there is now a preponderance of support from The IIA that internal auditors' mandate to remain independent does not prevent them from collaborating—and further, that coordination and collaboration across the three lines are critical for enabling us to better serve our organizations' objectives.

Placing Value at the Center of Risk Management

Recall how COSO and ISO define "risk": the possibility that events will occur and affect the achievement of objectives, or at minimum, create uncertainty around organizations' ability to achieve their objectives.

The crucial need now is to refocus everyone in the organization on the bigger-picture objectives behind risk management—value protection, realization, and creation—to ensure that risk management is seen not as the end, but rather as a key component of the means. When it comes to serving the greater purpose of creating and preserving value for stakeholders, nobody should be averse to collaboration.

In a 2022 LinkedIn article, Peter Bäckman observed:

> A risk-aware organization understands that ERM is a group effort. In a risk-aware culture, each member of the corporate community is empowered and equipped to recognize and act on anything they might perceive as risk. Organizational resilience cannot be siloed from department to department—it must be a unified effort across the company.[14]

With all that said, let me reiterate: discussions must remain respectful, so some organizations may need a different word to become comfortable moving forward. Consider the language that makes the most sense for your organization, be it collaboration, coordination, alignment, connection, or another word. Indeed, all of these terms are at the heart of the sustained value connected risk provides to organizations. You should choose the term that works for you.

Unfortunately, the big-picture reality is that all of the carefully worded professional standards, guidance, and directives in the world are unlikely to swiftly remove the ingrained hurdles to collaboration. To do that, we must travel a few steps further to understand the roots of the problem. Is the way we think about the "three lines" unduly contributing to the issue?

CHAPTER 8

Beyond the Three Lines Approach

As we've demonstrated, improving collaboration across all the risk teams faces challenges, from stubborn siloing to independence concerns and beyond. We won't surmount these hurdles without challenging our thinking and assumptions about how the key players in risk management work together.

I have great respect for The IIA's Three Lines Model and for how The IIA has meaningfully evolved the model over the years. I have often been part of these efforts. The time has come, however, to reconsider the model's effectiveness in enabling genuine collaboration between the three lines, taking a fresh look at its structure, language, and limitations. Amid these extraordinary risk conditions, the very concept of three distinct lines is increasingly a trip hazard.

It's also time to directly address one of the model's limitations. I've always felt that the Three Lines Model and its predecessors were largely written to—and from—an internal audit-centric perspective. Its structure essentially positions internal auditors as the "heroes" of risk management, ready to save the day by identifying risk management, control, and governance deficiencies everyone else has missed. While I am obviously a champion for internal auditing and the value it has historically provided, it is every bit as critical that second- and first-line functions are recognized as vital to effective risk management alongside internal audit.

Over the years, some risk and compliance professionals have privately called out that the Three Lines Model relegates them (albeit unintentionally) to seemingly less important roles. Further, InfoSec professionals have not been specifically acknowledged in the verbiage. While their inclusion is implied, it's time to explicitly acknowledge their essential presence as one of the vital risk and control oversight functions comprising the second line.

Since I myself was part of the model's evolution, I can confirm that The IIA embraced it with the best intentions. I can also confirm that The IIA is committed to continually evolving how the three lines work together to best serve the objectives of the organizations we serve; this commitment is evident in their 2020 revision of the model. With that spirit in mind, we begin by looking at where the model and its guidance originated and how it has evolved over the years. Then, I'll share my idea for a companion framework—the Connected Risk Model—to support a more aligned and collaborative approach to risk management.

The Origins of the Three Lines of Defense

While the exact source of the three lines' approach is a matter of debate, many sources agree on when and where the first Three Lines of Defense Model was published. It was embraced between 2008 and 2010 by the Federation of European Risk Management Associations (FERMA) and the European Confederation of Institutes of Internal Auditing (ECIIA) as guidance for the 8th EU Directive Art. 41 2b. Section 2b of the directive stated, "the audit committee shall, inter alia: monitor the effectiveness of the company's internal control, internal audit where applicable, and risk management systems."

FERMA and ECIIA's 2010 guidance explained the reason for its issuance, stating, "While this seems to be a rather simple statement, 'what to monitor' and 'how to monitor' are considerably more complex." Accordingly, the guidance aimed "to shed light on 'what' and 'how' to monitor" by providing an overview of the role and responsibilities regarding effective risk management and control assurance for the board/audit committee; CEO and senior management; operational management; and monitoring and assurance functions. It also clarified "the recommended interaction between internal control, risk management and internal audit" and suggested "good practices for board and audit committee oversight" regarding the risk management process, the internal control system, and the internal auditing function.[1]

To this end, the guidance included a Three Lines of Defense Model that illustrated these different responsibilities and interactions. At the center of the graphic were three large blue boxes—the three lines of defense—delineated as follows:

- **First line of defense:** Operational Management; Internal Controls
- **Second line of defense:** Risk Management; Compliance; Others
- **Third line of defense:** Internal Audit

Importantly, these "lines of defense" effectively separated the various parties involved in risk management into three distinct groups: the first line of defense owns and manages risks, the second line of defense oversees the effectiveness of risk management and controls implemented by the first line, and the third line of defense provides independent assurance on the effectiveness of risk management and controls.

The model also addressed oversight and external auditing. Two smaller blue boxes were shown above the three lines: "Senior Management" was shown extending the first and second lines, and "Board/Audit Committee" across the second and third lines. To the right of the third line, another small box represented "External Audit," with a solid line separating internal audit from external audit.

Dotted lines between the boxes representing the three lines of defense suggested both separation and permeability. There were no arrows or connectors between any of the boxes. The paper did, however, follow the model with brief explanations describing the responsibilities and interactions between the three lines. It also specifically mentioned external audit as a "fourth line of defense."

The IIA's 2013 Three Lines of Defense Model

As FERMA and ECIIA wrote in 2010, their model was "rapidly gaining universal recognition."[2] Indeed, The IIA built upon this framework to formally endorse the Three Lines of Defense Model in 2013.

I was president and CEO of The IIA at the time. The 2013 model's publication and widespread acceptance (especially within internal audit) marked a significant step forward in helping organizations understand how the various roles could work together to ensure robust governance and risk management. The IIA's 2013 position paper sharing the model explained our rationale (emphasis added):

> In twenty-first century businesses, it's not uncommon to find diverse teams of internal auditors, enterprise risk management specialists, compliance officers, internal control specialists, quality inspectors, fraud investigators, and other risk and control professionals working together to help their organizations manage risk. **Each of these specialties has a unique perspective and specific skills that can be invaluable to the organizations they serve**, but because duties related to risk management and control are increasingly being split across multiple departments and divisions, **duties must be coordinated carefully to assure that risk and control processes operate as intended**.
>
> It's not enough that the various risk and control functions exist—**the challenge is to assign specific roles and to coordinate effectively and efficiently among these groups so that there are neither "gaps" in controls nor unnecessary duplications of coverage**. Clear responsibilities must be defined so that each group of risk and control professionals understands the boundaries of their responsibilities and how their positions fit into the organization's overall risk and control structure.
>
> The stakes are high. Without a cohesive, coordinated approach, **limited risk and control resources may not be deployed effectively, and significant risks may not be identified or managed appropriately**. In the worst cases, communications among the various risk and control groups may devolve to little more than an ongoing debate about whose job it is to accomplish specific tasks.

To that end, the paper continued, the model "provides a simple and effective way to **enhance communications** on risk management and control **by clarifying essential roles and duties.**"[3]

We also envisioned The IIA's Three Lines of Defense Model as definitively illustrating where internal audit sits and how it provides value in an organization's overall governance and risk management framework. We knew it was critical to firmly establish internal audit's vital role in providing independent assurance, writing:

> Internal auditors provide the governing body and senior management with comprehensive assurance based on the highest level of independence and objectivity within the organization. This high level of independence is not available in the second line of defense. Internal audit actively contributes to effective organizational governance providing certain conditions—fostering its independence and professionalism—are met.[4]

The IIA's 2013 position paper also included more detailed language delineating each line's responsibilities, as well as advice regarding tailoring duties, responsibilities, and implementation to fit each organization's unique needs.

Deconstructing the Lines of Defense

The "lines of defense" concept was, of course, not unique to internal audit. It has been used in many other contexts to denote the presence of multiple protective barriers. For example:

- **Medieval castles** were designed with multiple lines of defense (e.g., moats, gates, towers), each protecting the next with the strategy that fewer and fewer attacking forces will permeate each line.
- In scientific circles, the term is used to describe the **immune system's "three lines of defense,"** operating like military defenses to keep out as many pathogens as possible.

As FERMA, ECIIA, and The IIA all recognized, the essential concept of different "lines of defense" was similarly apt for illustrating how risk management is intended to work. With all lines operating concurrently, organizations have at least three chances to identify, manage, and mitigate risk more effectively, thereby strengthening the organization's overall risk management. Notably, the term "defense" in the model's title also clearly emphasized the roles of the key players in protecting value—with little to no thought given to value creation.

As the 2013 position paper admitted, "In a perfect world, perhaps only one line of defense would be needed to assure effective risk management. In the real world, however, a single line of defense often can prove inadequate."[5] Accordingly, the model sought to showcase how the different groups responsible for risk management could organize and coordinate to become more effective in carrying out their responsibilities.

- **First line of defense:** Because management owns risks, they are responsible for identifying risks, and designing and implementing controls to mitigate risks.
- **Second line of defense:** Because risk management, compliance, and other second-line functions oversee the effectiveness of risk management, they are responsible for ensuring that risks are identified and the controls implemented by management are effective. If the first line misses anything, the second line does its best to catch it and support the first line in addressing it.
- **Third line of defense:** In providing independent assurance on risk management, internal audit is responsible for catching anything the first and second lines do not before it creates impairments (or worse) for the enterprise (e.g., a control weakness).

Beyond the three lines exists what I call the abyss—the space where external auditors, regulators, or markets are the ones who catch the issue, leading to potentially devastating impacts on the organization.

The IIA's 2020 "Three Lines Model"

The IIA provided a timely update to the Three Lines Model in 2020. The revision, which we envisioned as softening the concept of "defense," was widely recognized as an improvement.

The new model strived to remove some of the rigidity implied by the 2013 model that had manifested in the unfortunate siloing of internal audit, risk management, and compliance. That model had also seemed to reinforce internal auditors' hesitancy to provide first- and second-line functions with insights and recommendations on risk management design and implementation.

When The IIA announced the new model in July 2020, I was still CEO; in the press release, I described how the updates were intended to "modernize and strengthen application of the model to ensure its sustained usefulness and value." Accordingly, the release described how the refreshed model would help organizations "better identify and structure interactions and responsibilities of key players toward achieving more effective alignment, collaboration, accountability and, ultimately, objectives."[6]

The 2020 version, shown in Figure 8-1, included the following noteworthy revisions:

- The word "defense" was removed from the model's title.
- While we retained the "lines" terminology for the sake of familiarity and avoiding confusion, a footnote clarified that the lines "are not intended to denote structural elements but a useful differentiation in roles."
- Instead of the 2013 model's arrows proceeding in only one direction (signifying upward reporting to senior management and the governing body), the vertically oriented arrows now ran in both directions. As the graphic's language reflects, the intent was to suggest not only accountability and reporting, but also ongoing discussion, oversight, direction, delegation, and sharing of resources.
- We added a horizontal double-ended arrow between internal audit and "Management" (which now united the first and second lines below a single umbrella), explicitly indicating alignment, communication, coordination, and collaboration.
- We generalized the lines' descriptions, focusing on "roles" described in terms of activities.

Figure 8-1
The IIA's Three Lines Model (2020)

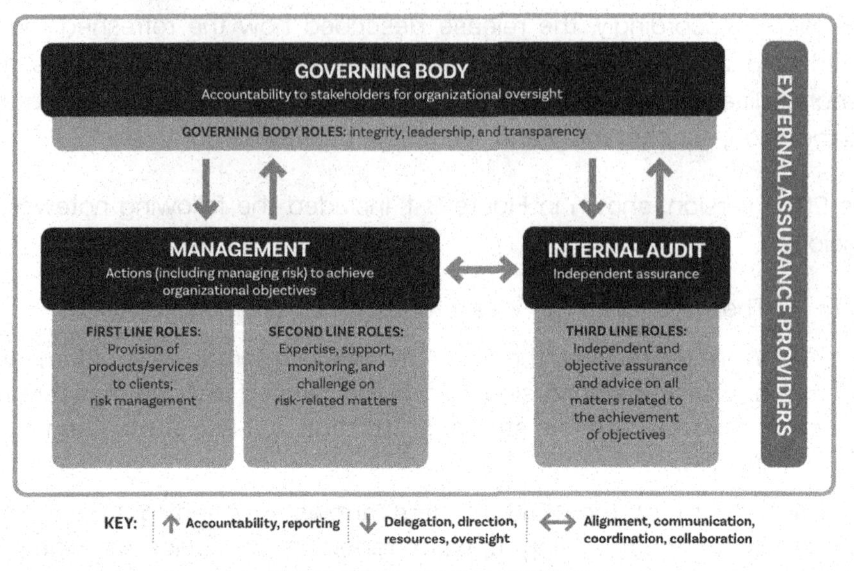

We also made revisions to the accompanying guidance—most significantly, to **Principle 6: Creating and protecting value**, which stated (emphasis added):

> **All roles working together collectively** contribute to the creation and protection of value when they are **aligned with each other** and with the prioritized interests of stakeholders. **Alignment of activities is achieved through communication, cooperation, and collaboration**. This ensures the reliability, coherence, and transparency of information needed for risk-based decision-making.[7]

This addition reflects a critical reality that the 2013 model and position paper did not adequately address. The 2013 paper indeed discussed the "what" of risk management in detail, focusing on roles and responsibilities, effective internal controls, alignment with goals and objectives, and so on. But the "why" was largely left unexplored, and the 2020 revision sought to remedy this need.

The "why" also happens to be the burning platform at the core of this book: organizations exist to achieve the objectives of preserving, enhancing, creating, and realizing value for stakeholders. Organizations will not achieve these objectives simply by protecting the value they already have.

By extension, risk and assurance teams that insist on working in isolation in their silos are not serving the ends of their organizations as effectively as they can. We all must be willing to connect across the three lines. This is the essence of connected risk.

The Side Effect of Separation and Silos

The IIA's 2013 Three Lines of Defense Model and 2020 Three Lines Model were valuable concepts that helped organizations refine their thinking about risk management. I give our 2013 efforts due credit for emphasizing communication between the three lines, and commend our 2020 revision for removing the outdated "defense" terminology and deliberate focus on improving alignment, communication, coordination, and collaboration.

In practice, however, the three lines have continued to operate largely independently and in silos, and the "defense" phrasing persists in many circles. Our 2013 position paper had declared, "Risk management normally is strongest when there are three separate and clearly identified lines of defense."[8] While our 2020 position paper made worthy efforts to amend this way of thinking, many key risk players have not moved past it, mistakenly believing that strength depends on separation.

Regrettably, this separation does not always create the connectivity and alignment that helps organizations be effective in identifying and managing risks. When everyone is focused on peering through their own narrow lenses, they are apt to miss a great deal.

Especially now. I began chapter 3 by using weather as an analogy to understand the risk conditions of permacrisis. I extend that analogy now by imagining your organization as a ship navigating stormy seas.

With risks emerging so quickly from so many directions, it is imperative to gather all hands on deck. Your organization has chosen one or more destinations (your business objectives); to complete the journey successfully, you need everyone together on the ship's navigation bridge, binoculars scanning in all directions. At the same time, each crew member must be actively monitoring the devices they have deployed to assess any areas they can't see directly, surveilling currents, depths, and weather; identifying shoals or other obstacles hidden below the surface; and anticipating coming storms or ships with courses intersecting yours. Most importantly, everyone must share their findings, warnings, and predictions with everyone else, forming as complete a picture as possible of overall conditions that enables the captain to plan and adjust the course accordingly.

You can't afford to ride into the eye of a hurricane or remain on a course that will cause you to collide with a freighter three times your size. Unfortunately, if the persistent separation between the three lines is allowed to continue, your organization is apt to do precisely that.

A New Model for a New World

In the press release accompanying The IIA's 2020 Three Lines Model, I also said, "The updated Three Lines Model addresses the complexities of our modern world."[9] I believed this at the time. As I spent the first several chapters of this book establishing, however, our world has changed dramatically since 2020.

Even though our 2020 guidance used a more connective tone that explicitly encouraged reaching across the lines, and posited that the lines exist only to show "useful differentiation in roles"[10]—there are still lines. Three lines do not suggest connection. The mathematical definition of "line" denotes a straight, one-dimensional figure extending infinitely in opposing directions. In math, "lines" do not meet; if they do, they are defined otherwise (e.g., as angles or shapes).

It may be time to cast off the concept of lines altogether to create a new conceptual structure. As chapter 1 outlined, COSO's ERM framework underwent exactly this type of evolution: the 2004 cube was updated in 2017 to the colorful, three-dimensional, intertwining ribbons resembling a DNA strand. As COSO's 2017 executive summary stated:

The updated Framework in COSO's publication:

- More clearly connects enterprise risk management with a multitude of stakeholder expectations
- Positions risk in the context of an organization's performance, rather than as the subject of an isolated exercise
- Enables organizations to better anticipate risk so they can get ahead of it, with an understanding that change creates opportunities, not simply the potential for crises

This update also answers the call for a stronger emphasis on how enterprise risk management informs strategy and its performance.

Note COSO's amplified emphasis on organizational context, strategy, and performance, connection with stakeholder expectations, and focus on "understanding that change creates opportunities."[11] The baseline message: ERM is not the end product, but rather the process by which organizations protect and create value for stakeholders. We can learn from COSO's example as we forge a new path toward a more connected, aligned, and outcomes-focused approach to risk management.

In the spirit of moving everyone in the organization forward along this path, I have been working on an entirely new conceptual framework—one that doesn't intend to replace the Three Lines Model, but rather supplement it. While I have consulted with several esteemed colleagues (both past and present) to develop the model you see here, I consider it a first incarnation that we can continue to develop together.

I call it the *Connected Risk Model* to stress its overarching goal: connecting and aligning teams around the shared objectives of value protection, creation, and realization, and making collaboration between them a foregone conclusion for effectively addressing the risk exposure gap.

As Figure 8-2 illustrates, each key risk player has a distinct, valid, respected purpose that remains unchanged. Management will always have to identify, assess, and implement appropriate controls to mitigate risk. Monitoring and oversight functions (e.g., risk management, compliance) will continue ensuring the effectiveness of risk management in the design and implementation of controls. InfoSec will continue safeguarding the organization's assets by assuring the confidentiality, integrity, and availability of information, and internal audit will persevere in providing independent, objective assurance on risk management effectiveness. The Connected Risk Model does not erase or diminish any of these vital responsibilities.

Figure 8-2
The Connected Risk Model

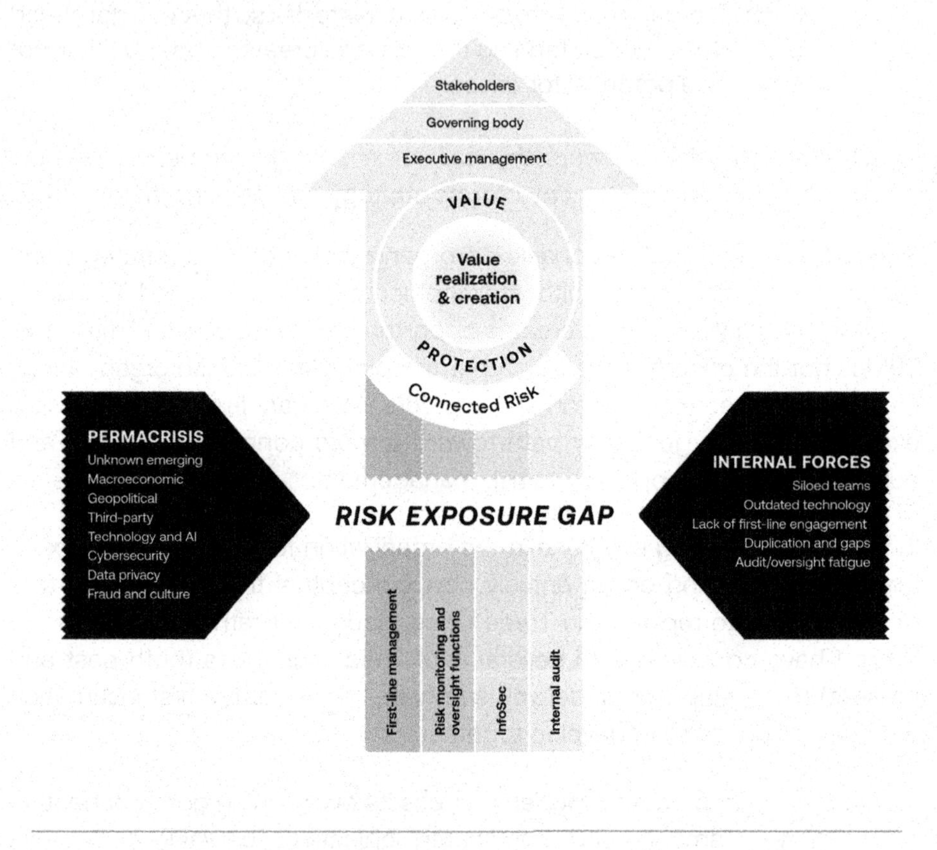

The risk exposure gap (created by the external and internal forces shown) is where these teams must come together. Whereas the graphic's lower section shows solid lines acknowledging teams' individual purposes, their continuation above the risk exposure gap is permeable. This is the point at which cross-functional collaboration, alignment, and connected data, people, processes, and technologies enable connected risk.

In turn, connected risk enables all teams to support their shared objective of value protection, without which value realization and creation are not possible. Think of value protection as the shell guarding the egg. Just as an egg cannot survive without its shell, value realization and creation are futile without value protection.

These activities—distinct purposes and shared objectives—occur under the watchful eye of executive management, who are then accountable to their respective governing bodies and stakeholders. The upward arrow symbolizes ongoing accountability, not only to executive management, governing bodies, and stakeholders but also to the overall objectives of value protection, realization, and creation.

In the Connected Risk Model, no role is set apart as the risk management "hero." The only heroes in permacrisis are those who band together across traditional lines, uniting their unique skills and perspectives to create—in Aristotle's immortal words—a whole that is greater than the sum of its parts.

Part 4

The Connected Risk Imperative

CHAPTER 9

Fostering Connected Risk Thinking

Up to this point, I have methodically made the case for why I believe connected risk is the right approach for transforming risk management to better meet the needs of the modern age. I have argued for softening the lines that have historically hindered effective collaboration and for emerging from our caves once and for all for the benefit of our organizations.

We now reach the most pressing item on our agenda: how can you embrace connected risk to achieve greater cross-functional collaboration and alignment? From this point forward, we'll explore guidance, strategies, and tactics for laying the groundwork to do exactly that.

This section is essentially a guide for spearheading connected risk in your organization. First, this chapter takes a journey from the general to the specific, starting with principles and driving forces and proceeding to foundational projects and strategies for evangelizing connected risk. Next, we'll explore the attributes of connected risk thinkers before considering the attributes of technology that enables a connected risk approach, helping you navigate common challenges and identify technologies that enable—not hinder—connection and collaboration. Lastly, we'll help you build a business case and perfect your pitch, positioning you to bring key stakeholders on board from across the organization.

However, as you plan your approach, recognize what you're up against: connected risk will be a sea change for most organizations. Laying the foundations begins with making a strong case for connected risk and taking catalyzing action to foster connected risk thinking in your organization. It requires becoming an "agent of change" to drive connected risk.

In 2021, my book, *Agents of Change: Internal Auditors in an Era of Disruption*, formally issued my call to action for internal auditors to become agents of change. Not even a year into the COVID-19 pandemic, standing at the precipice of an era of unprecedented disruptive change, I already had a deep sense that the internal audit profession needed to adapt, step up, and become catalysts for transformational change that creates value for our organizations.

That imperative has only deepened and widened. That's why this book expands that call to action across all three lines, charging everyone in the organization to take a hard look at how they must adapt. To effectively influence positive change, connected risk agents of change must come prepared with well-thought-out arguments, leading practices, and concrete ideas for getting started. Without further ado, let's arm you to be a connected risk agent of change.

Guiding Principles for Connected Risk

Understandably, many people are feeling the whiplash wrought by the exceedingly turbulent first half of the 2020s. I wouldn't fault anyone for growing somewhat weary of the change and disruption. In such times, it's tempting to cling to what's familiar, search for routes of relative safety, and hold tight to the core identities that give us the courage to keep moving forward. It's only natural to feel hesitant when someone shows up insisting that more change is needed.

It's also only natural to feel impugned when someone suggests we should do our jobs differently. Such views strike at the very bedrock of our personal and professional identities, whether intentionally or not.

People don't willingly sign onto change initiatives that appear to call into question their core identities. They're also slow to embrace change if they don't readily see its benefit for their day-to-day work, or worse, if they feel it somehow devalues what they do. Bear these truths in mind as you plan your approach. Specifically, as you start sowing the seeds of connected risk in your organization, make sure your end game is informed by respect, understanding, and flexibility. The following guiding principles can help lead the way.

1. Recognize the Professional Distinctions Between the Key Players

Each of the key players in connected risk brings to the table a different but equally valuable set of core competencies. For example:

First-line roles—given their overall responsibility for achieving the organization's objectives, managing risks that threaten those objectives, designing and implementing appropriate controls to manage risks, and ensuring legal, regulatory, and ethical compliance—have a unique perspective on how day-to-day risk management supports the organization in achieving its objectives. That said, as COSO's executive summary to its 2017 framework update suggests, "it is important for management to go further: to enhance the conversation with the board and stakeholders about using enterprise risk management to gain a competitive advantage."[1] All of these activities require management to engage in risk-based decision-making and resource allocation and application that are validated by second- and third-line professionals.

Risk managers bring a keen understanding of risk management theory and practice. They already appreciate the importance of understanding risk in the context of the organization's strategy and performance, and of meaningfully embedding risk management throughout the organization's governance, processes, activities, decision-making, policies, culture, and strategy. Notably, as COSO explains, ERM "enriches management dialogue by adding perspective to the strengths and weaknesses of a strategy as conditions change, and to how well a strategy fits with the organization's mission and vision."[2]

InfoSec professionals have deep knowledge of technology-related risks and a ready-made understanding of how their work fits into the bigger picture of the organization's value protection and creation objectives. After all, the information security profession is predicated on understanding how their work impacts the confidentiality, integrity, availability, authenticity, and resilience of the organization's data and systems.

Compliance professionals bring specialized expertise in assisting first-line teams to comply with laws, regulations, and ethical standards, enabling them to analyze and report on risk management effectiveness in these areas. Given the rapid pace of regulatory change in recent years, compliance professionals play a vital role in helping first-line teams identify, understand, and address the critical compliance risks impacting organizations.

Internal auditors offer broad professional skills and acumen in providing independent assurance and advice on organizations' risk management, governance, and internal control processes. This means they have a shrewd understanding of processes and standards, as well as wide-ranging knowledge and relationships across the organization. Internal auditors' objectivity and independence from management, coupled with their focus on continuous improvement, make them a valuable source of assurance, insight, and foresight on overall risk management.

2. Celebrate the Unique Strengths of All the Key Players

Connected risk does not aim to streamline risk management to the point where everyone possesses the same skill set. Rather, the power of connected risk comes from getting the key players working together while simultaneously celebrating the unique ways they're each able to leverage their acumen and experience.

Design connected risk roles and responsibilities so that they acknowledge and capitalize on each group's strengths. Make sure you're creating an environment in which all stakeholders feel their input, concerns, and feedback are valued, acknowledged, and leveraged by the other key players toward the collective benefit of the organization.

3. Reduce Anxiety about Greater Cross-Line Collaboration

As a long-time internal auditor, I understand the anxiety that can arise when people start talking about "collaboration." It's why I devoted much of chapter 8 to assuaging these concerns. At the end of the day, people's concerns and fears should never be dismissed or belittled. Rather, they should be respectfully heard, acknowledged, and resolved.

Changing how we think is no small feat. The next chapter is dedicated to this topic. Before people can change how they think, however, they need to clearly understand why the change is needed—and how they themselves play an important role in making change happen. You want them to embrace the core message behind connected risk: "By bringing my unique strengths, I contribute to my organization's collective ability to manage risk and protect and create value."

4. Understand and Take Advantage of Existing Crossover

Connected risk requires organizations to create and formalize roles, responsibilities, and communication channels that enable more effective collaboration. Luckily, this may not be as daunting a task as it sounds because there exists a high degree of crossover in risk-related responsibilities at many organizations. This is especially true in the case of CAEs. The IAF's *2024 North American Pulse of Internal Audit* finds that 84 percent of CAEs have responsibilities outside internal audit. For example:

- **Many CAEs have ERM responsibilities,** with the Pulse survey assessing that 31 percent of all CAEs surveyed have these responsibilities. Breaking these figures down by type of organization increases the percentages in two noteworthy cases: CAEs are responsible for ERM at 61 percent of privately held companies and 40 percent of publicly traded companies.
- **Many CAEs have SOX compliance program responsibilities,** with the Pulse survey assessing that 34 percent of all CAEs surveyed hold these responsibilities. The trend is much higher at publicly traded companies, which report that 69 percent of CAEs have SOX program responsibilities.
- **Many CAEs have other compliance/regulatory responsibilities,** with the Pulse survey showing that 22 percent of all CAEs surveyed have these responsibilities. This average rises to 25 percent at privately held companies and 34 percent at public sector companies, and dips to 19 percent at publicly traded companies.[3]

While you're highly unlikely to find internal audit taking on CISO responsibilities, the overall point stands: in bringing many of these groups together, organizations are typically not trying to coalesce across oceans and from separate continents. These professionals are already "collaborating" with themselves in many cases.

Consider creating a risk assurance map to determine which teams hold which responsibilities in your organization. A risk assurance map is a leading practice tool for identifying and coordinating your organization's various sources of assurance; we'll explain the process in more detail later in the chapter.

5. Nurture Key Relationships

Beyond building off existing crossover, nurture any collaboration that is already happening in your organization and identify opportunities to encourage collaboration between teams that have natural synergies. For example:

- **InfoSec and compliance** can share a controls library, control assessments, and testing results to drive efficiency for control owners during implementation and assessment; prioritize security controls based on shared universe of assets; and conduct risk assessments and quantify risk based on historical incident data.
- **InfoSec and risk management** can establish a shared risk taxonomy to provide end-to-end visibility and a single language for enterprise risk, and leverage risk impacts to help prioritize compliance and security efforts.
- **InfoSec and internal audit** can share risk reporting and insights, and work together on information security controls documentation and testing work, managing issue remediation processes, and facilitating IT risk assessments.
- **Compliance and risk management** can share issues to improve visibility, better understand issue impact, and provide unified, inventory-level visibility for stakeholders to facilitate a more risk-aware culture.
- **Compliance and internal audit** can team on compliance risk assessments, share insights and updates on systemic or emerging compliance issues, and strive for increased alignment in board and management communications.
- **Internal audit and risk management** can explore linking audit plans and risk assessments, sharing risk registers, teaming to monitor strategic risks, sharing resources who have availability, aligning board and management communications and reporting, and cross-leveraging staff and overall expertise.
- **Internal audit and SOX compliance** can create and manage a shared issues list, identify and eliminate work (e.g., certain audit reports or processes) that isn't needed, and work with external auditors to increase their reliance on management's work.

6. Embrace a Talent Management Strategy That Embeds Collaboration

Collaboration is a compulsory foundation for connected risk and a key ingredient in connected risk thinking. While the next chapter considers this need in more detail, the salient point here is that management and the board must set clear expectations that collaboration is a requirement within every professional's job description. This necessitates an outcomes-based talent management strategy that embeds the expectation of collaboration.

Make sure onboarding, policies, training, values, and leadership communications consistently convey that collaboration is a key capacity upon which every employee's performance will be assessed—and that caves are off limits if they wish to be rated as effective in their roles, much less as "exceeding" expectations.

8. Speak Truth to Power

At this point in time, the impetus for most connected risk approaches originates not from the board or C-suite, but from within the ranks of the second and third lines. These connected risk agents of change recognize a need and have the courage to speak up. This is particularly true in organizations where resistance to change prevails.

As previously noted, many professionals within the traditional three lines are territorial about their responsibilities. Challenging the conventional ways of doing things requires courage—particularly if executives in charge of the other lines are powerful forces within the organization.

The need to speak truth to power in such a situation may seem obvious. The reality is that it doesn't happen as much as it should. Often, the organization's culture doesn't encourage or reward speaking up—or worse, the culture is toxic enough that people worry that speaking up would be resented or even cost them their job. At times, it may simply come down to hesitancy to stick one's neck out or cause others discomfort.

Decidedly, the challenges facing organizations in the twenty-first century are not for the faint of heart. This is precisely why agents of change must find the fortitude to speak up when change is needed. In my experience, speaking truth to power is possible in nearly any circumstance if one proceeds with respect, kindness, openness, and a focus on the facts.

Understanding Connected Risk Catalyzing Factors

How does the push for connected risk begin in most organizations? Under what circumstances do organizations decide to invest in connected risk, and who typically leads the charge? In his role as AuditBoard's Field Chief Audit Executive, Tom O'Reilly most often sees the following four driving forces leading the push.

1. A Substantive Adverse Risk Event Occurs

Said O'Reilly, "Whether the event is a common data breach or an uncommon 'black swan' type of event, the impact is large enough that a member of executive management or the board has a knee-jerk reaction to push the organization to significantly uplevel its risk management." While they may not have a detailed understanding of what went wrong, where, or why, they have a clear sense that risk management must improve.

2. First-Line Pain Points Become Excessive

The first-line leaders feeling the pain begin pushing executive management to help them find solutions. "For example, perhaps an IT manager responsible for responding to all of the organization's controls and audit functions is feeling extreme audit fatigue after being asked for the same information multiple times in multiple formats," explained O'Reilly. In these situations, as complaints mount, one or more C-suite leaders decide to take action to investigate the problem and find a solution.

3. Risk Resource Constraints Demand Change

The organization is feeling the risk exposure gap without necessarily calling it that by name. Consensus is growing that the organization must make better use of its limited risk management resources. Often this leads to a search for enabling technologies that help reduce the administrative burden of the organization's assurance, risk management, and controls programs. "Connected risk becomes a tool that allows people to do less administrative work, and more of what they were hired to do—which is to assess, analyze, communicate, and strategize how to best help the organization protect itself from threats or take advantage of opportunities," said O'Reilly.

4. A Leader Brings a Vision for Transformation

Someone in the organization has a compelling vision for transforming risk management. The vision most often originates with a modern audit or risk leader who appreciates the concept of alignment between a company's objectives, risks, controls, and assurance all working together. As O'Reilly explains, "Having achieved some success in improving alignment of the areas under their remit—for example, sharing controls, risk assessments, and a risk universe between SOX, internal audit, and ERM—they begin sharing their connected risk success story, advocating for its benefits, evangelizing the need, and potentially oversee or even architect a connected risk approach for their company."

Every single one of these scenarios boils down to one key ingredient: someone in the organization has the courage to speak up and push for change.

Anticipating Common Reasons for NOT Investing

Clearing the path for transformation sometimes necessitates proactively clearing real or perceived obstacles. Accordingly, it's helpful to understand the most common reasons organizations cite for not investing in a connected risk strategy. O'Reilly has most often heard three main reasons.

1. They Don't See the Need

Neither executives nor the board perceive that a different strategy is necessary, justifying it by saying things like "We haven't had any catastrophic events yet" or "We're doing okay without it so far."

The language betrays the truth: despite any feigned confidence, they know there is a high probability something could happen to change their tune. To help them see the light before circumstances make it mandatory, consider sharing external resources such as WEF's *Global Risks Report*, Protiviti/NC State's *Executive Perspectives on Key Risks*, and other risk surveys or benchmarking relevant to your industry.

2. They Don't Have the Time

While teams say they understand the importance of a new risk management strategy, their time and efforts are allocated to other priorities (e.g., integrating a new acquisition, entering a new market).

To overcome this impediment, call out that a connected risk approach ultimately frees up the organization's key risk players to spend less time on non value-added activities and more time on higher-value work. In other words, investing time now on connected risk can open more bandwidth in the long term.

3. They Want a Proven Blueprint with Clear Instructions

In this case, teams understand the importance of connected risk and express a willingness to invest resources. They are nonetheless hesitant to move forward without a well-defined blueprint showing them the way. At the end of the day, they don't want to put themselves—and their reputations—on the line without more certainty about implementation.

As chapter 11 explores in detail, there is no one-size-fits-all approach to connected risk because implementation varies based on each organization's data, technology, and resource needs. Fortunately, O'Reilly has proven tactics that are excellent first steps for any organization. These initial projects can build support, demonstrate value, and get more of the organization onboard before implementation begins in earnest.

Lay the Groundwork with Four Foundational Projects

Anyone requesting transformative change should come equipped with at least some ideas about how to make it happen. The following are four key projects recommended by O'Reilly that you could suggest or spearhead to build the foundation for connected risk in your organization.

1. Data Governance Review

The longtime silos that exist in most organizations also create challenges around teams speaking different languages and using inconsistent taxonomies to define, assess, and prioritize risk. Clearly, this approach does not lend itself to unified or aligned outcomes. Further, the data organizations create tends to be largely unstructured, and efforts to segment, label, and tag data are often insufficient. As a result, much of the data goes unused, receding into various databases that don't connect.

Why it's necessary: To work more closely together, we must begin by sharing information and creating a common set of definitions. The overall goal is a unified data core that is up-to-date, reliable, and readily available to the stakeholders who need access to it. Accordingly, the first project O'Reilly recommends focuses on identifying and aligning your organization's key data.

Outcome: The outcome of this project is a baseline understanding of how your key data is being collected, shared, stored, and protected.

What to do: Create an inventory documenting all of your organization's key data, which typically includes intellectual property (IP) and other data that if lost, stolen, or destroyed, would have a significant negative impact on your business. Detail the data's location (i.e., network or physical location), who has access to the data, and any controls protecting and monitoring it.

2. Risk Assurance Mapping

Risk assurance activities extend across the organization and beyond, to external stakeholders such as consultants, external auditors, and regulators. Consequently, the second step O'Reilly recommends is building a risk assurance map: an inventory of the people and processes responsible for providing assurance around your organization's risks. Assurance mapping is also recommended in Standard 9.5 Coordination and Reliance.[4]

Why it's necessary: Connected risk is all about improving how we collaborate, enabling professionals across all lines to identify and leverage opportunities to learn from and leverage each other's expertise, insights, and work. A risk assurance map shines a bright spotlight on these opportunities.

Outcome: The outcome of this project is a visual representation that documents all of the assurance activities the organization has carried out in the past and scheduled in the future, thereby revealing any gaps, areas of overlap, or duplicative coverage. Beyond bringing to light any key risk areas where assurance capabilities are needed, this exercise can help reveal where your organization may be able to increase coordination and reliance.

What to do: Create a map of your organization's risk assurance activities, making sure to agree upon scope in advance. Assurance maps can be completed at varying levels of detail, depending on your goals in creating the map. O'Reilly's recommendation is to start with the key risks your organization has documented (likely from your ERM program), solicit feedback from risk owners on which internal and external assurance and advisory teams provide assurance over each area, and document the controls, workflows, processes, strategies, and projects these teams have for each risk area.

3. Technology and Maturity Assessment

The first two projects focused on aligning data and teams. Next, O'Reilly recommends creating an inventory of your organization's technology systems to assess the capabilities, limitations, and opportunities they offer.

Why it's necessary: Technology is a necessary component for any connected risk approach. If your existing technology systems don't enable you to easily share data across applications, it may be time to implement a system that does. As the next chapter discusses in more detail, connected risk is predicated on having a unified data core that enables not only data sharing but also consolidated reporting, access to real-time data and insights, and ideally a shared control environment.

Outcome: The outcome of this project is an inventory of all the audit, risk, compliance, and InfoSec technologies used in your organization, as well as an assessment of your organization's ability to connect internal and external data sources and share data across applications.

What to do: Inventory all audit, risk, compliance, and InfoSec technologies (including any AI programs) currently being used in your organization. Document and assess each application's ability to share data and the level of effort, resources, and costs required to periodically update each application's data.

4. Shared Risk Definitions

As we've mentioned, risk and assurance groups that have been regularly retreating to their caves often rely on different definitions and taxonomies to define, categorize, and prioritize the same risks. The risk assurance mapping project (see #2) will have identified the teams whose definitions and scoring systems need aligning. As a result, the last foundational project

O'Reilly recommends is creating a set of shared risk definitions and a single taxonomy that the different groups agree to use going forward.

Why it's necessary: Connected risk depends on everyone using the same taxonomy to assess and quantify risk, providing a clearer view of which risks genuinely matter most.

Outcome: The outcome of this project is a shared risk taxonomy that relies on common definitions of risk and a unified approach to quantifying and assessing risk.

What to do: Identify the various rating systems used to score risks (e.g., color coding, stoplights, high/medium/low), how each score is defined, what risk attributes are considered in assessments, and what KRIs teams are using. Agree on a single rating system, a shared set of definitions and KRIs, and common attributes to use in future assessments.

Evangelize Connection and Collaboration for Value Creation

We've repeatedly touched on this message because it is genuinely foundational to any successful connected risk program. Once your four foundational projects are complete, it is assuredly time to evangelize the value of connected risk through a concerted and strategic effort to coach across all three lines. Chapter 12 shares specific ideas for communicating the value of connected risk.

Your outreach should be guided by what makes sense for your organization, role, and relationships. For example, second- or third-line teams may decide to start by approaching their counterparts. A CAE with ERM or SOX responsibilities could begin by coordinating between those two groups, suggesting a unified risk and controls matrix and shared issue tracking as first steps. A risk manager who has a good relationship with a member of the compliance team might initiate a conversation about sharing controls or risk assessments in relevant areas. A CISO could approach the ERM team about using ERM insights to prioritize and drive security efforts.

O'Reilly particularly suggests collaborations involving InfoSec. Due to the well-understood importance of cybersecurity and data security in many organizations, many CISOs operating in the current environment are actively seeking ways to improve their control environments, increase coverage, address gaps, or reduce their administrative burden. Accordingly, they may be looking for help from teams with expertise in creating and documenting the organization's risks and controls. (Not all InfoSec teams have this experience, and not all CISOs want the responsibility to maintain documentation evidencing that risk and controls work is performed as needed.) Plus, as O'Reilly advised, "If you get information security onboard, it's likely to be easier to get meetings with other second-line teams in the organization."

Of course, it's also worth approaching first-line individuals or teams. Successfully implementing connected risk requires enlisting like-minded champions at several levels of the organization. Chapter 6 shared a list of pain points common to organizations feeling the impact of the risk exposure gap, calling out problems such as duplication of effort and audit fatigue, lost productivity and limited efficiency, gaps in risk coverage, poor data quality and availability, lack of risk visibility and context, lack of real-time risk identification, and several others. Anyone in the organization naming these pain points is likely to be a receptive audience.

Whatever your planned outreach, make sure to ground all conversations by concentrating on the benefits that connected risk can bring to their team, and the central importance of all teams' shared purpose relative to risk management: protecting, creating, and sustaining value for the organization and its stakeholders. Everyone must work together toward this singular outcome. We're in such a disruptive period that if everyone is content to identify and monitor risks on their own, they won't be nearly as adept at capturing the organization's full risk portfolio. To do better, we must embrace partnerships.

As Paul Sobel, former COSO chairman expressed:

> "The end outcome is organizational success, however you define that. And no individual—not the CEO, CFO, or anyone else—can drive that by themselves. You can inspire others. You can advise. You can train. But no individual can do it by themselves. That's why I've had very good relationships with CROs in organizations where I was the CAE. It helped

that I had a good background in it, so I could speak their language when I walked in the door.

But I also always took the approach—and then they took the same approach with me—that I'm gonna help you do a better job by whispering in your ear, giving you ideas, and I expect you to do the same to me. Because together, the whole is greater than the sum of its parts. Compliance rolls into that, and some of the other second-line functions can roll into that as well. We are all here to help this organization to be successful, and if I have ideas that you end up taking credit for because they fall under your umbrella, so be it. My thinking was that at some point it gets reciprocated, and that I'll be recognized and rewarded to an appropriate extent in the long run.

But for now, the question is: how can I help the company be more successful? It gets back to humility. It's a competitive business world, and so many people are thinking that they have to stand out. And they kind of forget that the best way to stand out is to help with the bigger picture, as opposed to standing out as an individual at a point in time."

CHAPTER 10

Attributes of Connected Risk Thinkers

Reimagining risk management requires us to embrace new ways of thinking—not only about risk itself, but also about how we think about the work we do and the outcomes we achieve. As I emphasized in the previous chapter, the effectiveness of any connected risk approach relies on fostering connected risk thinking throughout the organization. It is, therefore, paramount for the architects of this approach to have an in-depth understanding of what this thinking is (and is not).

This chapter endeavors to unpack the attributes of connected risk thinkers. How are they wired, and in what ways do they think differently? What sets them apart from traditional thinkers? Most important, how can someone new to these ideas aspire to connected risk thinking?

Connected risk thinkers possess many of the traits of "trusted advisors" and "agents of change" that I have explored in my other books. They also tend to possess a "genetically risk-centric" mindset that fuels their passion for connected risk management. After extensive interactions with connected risk thinkers and my observations of them, I have compiled seven attributes I believe they share.

1. Connected Risk Thinkers Focus on Strategic Outcomes over Tactical Outputs

As mentioned in chapter 7, traditional risk management players often focus on outputs as a measure of quality and performance. A risk manager points to how many risks they listed in their risk register and how often they updated it. An internal auditor proudly boasts about how many audit reports or findings they issued. Compliance professionals track the number of regulatory requirements they are monitoring and their current status. This comes about partly because professionals have been historically incentivized and rewarded based on these types of metrics, leading to a preponderance of quantitative outputs that can be easily measured and tracked. After all, as the old saying goes, what gets measured gets done!

This output-focused mentality also reflects thinking about risk management as an end rather than a means. After all, none of these outputs on their own indicates that the organization makes a profit, delivers value to stakeholders, or otherwise achieves its strategic objectives. Risk management adds little value without achieving outcomes—the end for which risk management is ultimately needed. Countless companies with exceptional internal audit, risk management, and compliance functions have failed because their work was tactically good but strategically disconnected.

Unsurprisingly, a mindset that emphasizes "what I do" rather than "what I achieve" sometimes results in risk and assurance teams failing to gain substantial stakeholder alignment or engagement. This may be because these teams are seen as "reporting" rather than "achieving." Reporting is only valuable insofar as it enables the organization to make decisions, take action, and achieve results.

Operating with a connected risk mindset means focusing on outcomes that drive value, decision-making, performance, and competitive advantage. When an outcomes-oriented approach is aligned with the organization's strategic objectives, there's no question of your value to the business. You are not "reporting," but rather "achieving."

In sum, connected risk thinkers recognize that all organizations exist to achieve objectives—and appreciate that the strategies organizations use to achieve their objectives are inevitably fraught with risks. Consequently, connected risk thinkers focus on strategic outcomes, striving to help their organizations navigate not only operational, compliance, financial, and technology risks, but strategic risks as well. They leverage their extraordinary risk acumen to recognize and understand the systems that define and influence the organization's goals and direction, and to pursue a strategic role on behalf of their organization. They know that progress necessitates an often disruptive and visionary mindset. As John F. Kennedy wrote, "There are risks and costs to action. But they are far less than the long-range risks of comfortable inaction."

2. Connected Risk Thinkers Champion the Relationship between Risk and Opportunity

Traditional thinking about risk management too often views risk as inherently negative—something to be avoided or mitigated at all costs. Conversely, connected risk thinkers embrace risk in all its dimensions. Yes, some risks must be avoided. But some risks are worth leaning into as paths to opportunities and innovation.

Connected risk thinkers possess a keen understanding of the relationship between risk and opportunity. They appreciate that organizations must take risks, and know that risks involve the possibility that actions or events will negatively impact the achievement of objectives or create the potential for loss, harm, or other adverse outcomes. They also readily see the possibility that an action or event will positively impact the achievement of objectives, offering the potential for gain, improvement, or other favorable outcomes.

When risk and assurance teams are guided by connected risk thinking, they are able to play a pivotal role in helping their organizations determine their risk appetites to achieve their strategic objectives. They become trusted advisors who help first-line teams make risk-informed strategic decisions about where to go, where to turn, when to turn around, and when to take a detour rather than the straighter path.

3. Connected Risk Thinkers Thrive on Collaboration

As prior chapters illustrate, traditional risk management thinking often results in disconnected teams operating in silos and keeping other teams at arm's length. These teams may genuinely believe that the separation allows them to do their best work, or that staying in one's lane or cave helps establish and protect credibility, objectivity, and independence while magnifying the specific value one provides. After all, if you came out of your cave with an idea, it's obviously yours alone.

This mindset tends to see siloed identities and structures as helping to create and define individual success. The focus on what "I" can do often manifests as a binary perspective that there's a finite "us" and an opposing "them."

Connected risk thinking focuses on connecting and aligning with a cross-organizational "we," widening the definition of "team" to include the entire organization. This way of thinking emphasizes the common goal shared by everyone in the organization, regardless of where they sit. While each key player has a distinct purpose, everyone shares a common objective: helping the organization achieve its goals. As Michael Jordan—inarguably one of the greatest basketball players of all time—is often quoted as saying, "Talent wins games, but teamwork and intelligence win championships."

Indeed, connected risk thinkers understand that they can achieve more by collaborating across traditional lines. For example, they quickly see how agreeing on a shared language and taxonomy—one of the foundational projects outlined in the previous chapter—will enable them to get more done and provide more value. They appreciate that unifying data and sharing insights will improve their understanding of the organization's overall risk management, positioning them to be more effective in their roles.

To put it bluntly, connected risk thinkers are willing to get comfortable using the word "collaboration."

4. Connected Risk Thinkers Are Relationship-Centric

I've shown how traditional risk management thinking tends to focus on and value "lines of defense" over the necessary points of interconnection between the lines: the relationships that help all three lines succeed in their common purpose.

One of the common traits I have explored in my books, *Trusted Advisors* and *Agents of Change*, is that these men and women possess outstanding relationship acumen. They naturally forge and sustain relationships based on respect, trust, and common goals, which describes connected risk thinkers to a "T." They realize that silos can be "death traps" for innovation and progress and have no interest in spending their valuable time hiding at the bottom of their silo or in the recesses of a cave. They invest in building strong, resilient relationships because they know they are foundational not only to getting good work done, but also to influencing and inspiring meaningful change.

5. Connected Risk Thinkers Are Wired for Two-Way Communication and Knowledge Sharing

Every organization does its best to recruit and retain the brightest people. Unfortunately, this can result in the common challenge wherein too many people genuinely believe they're the smartest ones in the room. They come in with strong, inflexible opinions, and don't truly listen to others' perspectives.

In connected risk thinking, humility is key. Connected risk thinkers genuinely appreciate how much they can learn from others. As financier and political advisor Bernard Baruch wrote, "Most of the successful people I've known are the ones who do more listening than talking."

Connected risk thinkers also understand that without bona fide communication, genuine connection cannot and does not occur. There's no way to agree on a risk mitigation strategy or understand which risks other groups are prioritizing. There's no way to learn from and effectively leverage each other's work. Connected risk thinkers don't just strive to make their own voices heard, but rather to ensure effective two-way communication that makes sure everyone's voices are heard and understood. This includes ensuring and emphasizing the audience's comprehension, interest, and benefit. I like to quote George Aubrey, the VP and Chief Auditor of Lenovo, to drive this point home.

> You can be the best technical auditor ever created when it comes to determining precisely what is at risk, identifying related key controls, designing the best tests, and drawing the right conclusions. But if you're unable to communicate to stakeholders in a way that drives change, you're like the proverbial tree that falls in the forest—no one hears.[1]

6. Connected Risk Thinkers Are Tech Savvy and Tech Fearless

Some risk and assurance professionals perform their work today in much the same way they did when I became an internal audit professional nearly 50 years ago. Human beings tend to be creatures of habit. Human beings who wish to remain relevant and demonstrate value in the age of AI, however, need to embrace technology to help them adapt and innovate how they perform their work.

When I joined the internal audit profession in 1975, the most sophisticated technology available to us was a 10-key calculator, and we maintained our data on 16-column paper pads. The work we could do was limited by our physical locations, the modes and speed by which we could communicate, and the fact that when we left the office each day, security and confidentiality dictated that we rarely took work home. Human workers were limited by a lack of technology.

Now, the reverse statement seems increasingly accurate: technology is limited by human workers. Though technology now grants us the capacity to work with nearly anyone at any time, anywhere in the world, with virtually no limitations on our computing power and communication speed, it's the humans who can't keep up.

It's nonetheless critical we try. Teams that dedicate themselves to adopting innovative approaches and methods—generally embracing technology to do so—tend to have a significantly greater impact than those that do not. We must embrace change in what we do and how we do it. Being open to change enables us to have a hand in choosing what we want change to look like.

For example, it is particularly important to explore the opportunities AI presents for our roles. AI can act as a capacity multiplier and accelerant for research, writing, report creation, documentation (e.g., risk or issue authoring), audit planning, risk assessments, certain testing and scanning tasks, data analysis, framework adoption, fraud detection, and so much more. Of course, AI adoption must be carefully managed, and it is imperative to ensure AI is being used securely and in accordance with organizational policies. In fact, if your organization is lagging behind in establishing AI governance, that's another key opportunity for risk management teams to step up.

7. Connected Risk Thinkers Excel in Their Roles—and Embrace the Need for Transformation

Traditional risk management thinkers are less inclined to challenge the status quo. They don't see it as their role to enact change and may be wary of crossing lines. They likely enjoy the "peace and quiet" of working alone.

Connected risk thinkers understand the need for continual improvement in their own roles and within the larger organization. They typically excel in performing their current responsibilities, often taking the initiative to improve their own processes. They understand that they're unlikely to convince others of the need to transform their processes if they aren't willing to first optimize their own.

By extension, connected risk thinkers understand the imperative to transform risk management to better meet the needs of the modern age. They understand—or at minimum, are starting to understand—that we must change how we think about and approach risk management to create organizations that can remain relevant and resilient in permacrisis.

As outlined in the previous chapter, connected risk initiatives typically originate for one of two reasons:

- **Top-down.** The push emanates from the board or management, who have grown frustrated at the lack of alignment or connection between the various teams providing them with information, insight, and guidance. They see a need for these teams to connect and align, helping avoid the confusion of providing oversight or making decisions based on conflicting information.
- **Bottom-up.** More often, someone in the business—often an ambitious second- or third-line leader—sees connected risk as an opportunity to make an impact. They've identified the need to be better but may lack how-to knowledge.

This challenge is not unfamiliar for many audit, risk, compliance, and InfoSec professionals. Given the nature of these roles, they often ask themselves, "Who am I to tell the audit committee, board, or management how to do their jobs?"

The IIA acknowledges and appreciates the balancing act that second- and third-line functions undertake daily. The new Standard 9.5 Coordination and Reliance (also referenced in chapter 7), addresses it head on, with the "Requirements" reading in part:

> The chief audit executive must coordinate with internal and external providers of assurance services and consider relying upon their work. Coordination of services minimizes duplication of efforts, highlights gaps in coverage of key risks, and enhances the overall value added by providers.
>
> If unable to achieve an appropriate level of coordination, the chief audit executive must raise any concerns with senior management and, if necessary, the board.[2]

In other words, The IIA is doing exactly what connected risk thinking recommends: setting the clear expectation that risk and assurance providers must work together—and that if they don't, the CAE must bring the lack of coordination to the attention of management and possibly the board. While those conversations will not be easy, they are crucial to moving forward with more effective risk management.

This is why it's vital to provide professionals across all three lines with the tools they need to have a productive conversation about risk management transformation at any level of the organization: the very reason I am writing this book. Opening the door to transformation may mean empowering a second- or third-line professional to approach an influential first-line leader. It could also be the reverse, with a first-line leader approaching their CRO, CAE, CCO, or CISO to say, "Let's look at this together. I think this could solve some of our problems."

Whatever the situation, coming equipped with a connected risk mindset—and a commitment to instilling it throughout your organization—is a fantastic place to start. For a connected risk mindset to have a real impact on improving risk management, however, effective leverage of technology is essential.

CHAPTER 11

Technology—From Impediment to Enabler

Organizations have developed many proven and reliable methods for enhancing and transforming business operations. Technology can help people scale those methods. As Apple co-founder Steve Jobs said, "What a computer is to me is the most remarkable tool that we have ever come up with. It's the equivalent of a bicycle for our minds."

For those of you who don't know the history of bicycles, let's be clear: the invention of the bicycle absolutely changed the world. In the 1890s, with the advent of the bicycle, lower- and middle-income people—and women, who were often not permitted to operate vehicles—were newly able to move from place to place more quickly, easily, cheaply, and freely than ever before. It enabled societal change, entrepreneurial opportunity, and industrial innovation. That said, a bicycle alone can do nothing without someone choosing its destination and employing their body and brain to power it there.

In other words, technology alone won't fix your organization's problems. Technology is simply a tool that can be strategically deployed to enhance how people and practices work. That's why it's essential to approach your risk management transformation with a balanced and integrated focus on people, practices, and platform. For example, as the prior chapter emphasized, engendering a culture that embraces a connected risk mindset is an absolutely fundamental aspect of risk management transformation. No organization will be successful if its culture does not recognize risk's unpredictability, peril, and potential.

Your connected risk approach will look different from the next organization's approach based on the needs, preferences, capabilities, and goals of the people, processes, and data it's designed to empower and connect. These considerations will help to inform your choice and configuration of technology. Accordingly, this chapter explores what connected risk technology is, what it isn't, and how to determine what connected risk looks like for your organization.

Connected Risk and IRM

Before diving in, I'd like to address a question I sometimes hear when I talk about connected risk: "isn't connected risk the same thing as IRM?" Connected risk and integrated risk management (IRM) do have noteworthy similarities. There are, however, key differences between them.

Gartner defines IRM as "the combined technology, processes, and data that serves to fulfill the objective of enabling the simplification, automation, and integration of strategic, operational, and IT risk management across an organization."[1] IRM is a proven road map for a data-driven, organization-spanning approach to risk management. It aims to proactively improve risk management and risk-based decision-making by understanding risk more holistically, in alignment with the organization's strategy and risk appetite.

This should all sound wonderfully familiar because IRM is the bedrock upon which connected risk is built. Connected risk, however, takes IRM a significant step further, mandating the connection of teams, data, controls, and processes to supercharge collaboration and make the most of the organization's collective capabilities. Whereas IRM places much of its focus on integrating data and reporting, connected risk adds vital layers of alignment, collaboration, and technology enablement that empower organizations to operate with greater agility, clarity, and a more accurate, real-time view on risk.

Furthermore, connected risk is emerging in an era in which software capabilities have rapidly advanced to empower teams with richer insights and enhanced collaboration. Connected risk is fully realized when generative AI, intelligent automation, and advanced analytics can proactively suggest content, map frameworks, provide insights, and encourage connections across teams. In short, connected risk fulfills an entirely new vision for how purpose-built, intelligent technology can transform an organization.

Indeed, how technology is used is a fundamental difference between IRM and connected risk. IRM doesn't define specific requirements for the technologies used to support it. Connected risk, on the other hand, stipulates minimum requirements for its supporting technologies—without which its objectives cannot be achieved.

Addressing the Roadblocks of Legacy Technologies

Before we explore what connected risk technology is, it's important to understand that technology can be both an enabler and an impediment. Some technologies can actually create obstacles to communication and collaboration—and such obstacles are surprisingly common in many legacy technologies.

Why are so many organizations saddled with technologies that prevent teams from working together effectively? As outlined in chapter 7, part of the problem originated in the functional silos that emerged and hardened over the years. Technology companies built solutions that were specific to the needs of each function. Then, as these solutions were improved and fine-tuned over the years to better meet function-specific needs, many teams quite understandably began to view these purpose-built solutions as indispensable to their work.

The problem is that most of these technologies don't connect or share data. They may perform their intended purposes quite well for one team, but their capabilities and capacity for customization tend to be limited. Further, they typically don't account for the collaboration needed to achieve connected risk.

This is precisely why, over the years, some of the smarter players in the technology space have acquired several of these purpose-built but limited technologies. These players can thus claim to have all three lines protected and supported. On the surface, this may indeed appear to be the case. The reality is that the software often doesn't work together, or that "working together" requires the use of expensive APIs, resource-intensive manual uploads, or additional software resources to support real-time data feeds between applications. Furthermore, this piecemeal approach limits how advanced technologies such as generative AI can operate because such capabilities require a truly unified data and software architecture.

In the end, many of these legacy governance, risk, and compliance (GRC) technologies fail to meet users' needs at the functional level. What's more, many of these technologies' capabilities go unused.

Also contributing to the problem: most organizations have taken a piecemeal approach toward technology selection and implementation. As new technologies emerged and gained popularity, different functions bolted on solution after solution. Sometimes they did so with the permission and knowledge of the organization's central IT function. Sometimes they did so without, as "shadow IT." The result, in many cases, is a "frankensteined" framework that very much has the capacity to come back to haunt its creators.

Further, even when organizations have elected to invest in a GRC or IRM platform with the stated goals of centralizing and coordinating management of key business activities, the way these systems are implemented may fail to deliver true connectivity. These solutions often entrust organizations to implement and design connectivity themselves, selling the capacity for customization without providing sufficient guidance or vision to achieve proper integration. Is it any surprise that most teams end up approaching implementation from the perspectives of their distinct silos, primarily looking out for their own needs and interests?

Again, your "bicycle" does nothing without you deciding where that bicycle needs to go, at what speed, and with what purpose. To ensure you select and successfully implement the right technology to enable your connected risk approach—technology capable of being an enabler rather than an impediment—your approach must be similarly deliberate. As former Microsoft CEO Bill Gates is credited with saying, "The first rule of any technology used in a business is that automation applied to an efficient operation will magnify the efficiency. The second is that automation applied to an inefficient operation will magnify the inefficiency."

What Is Connected Risk Technology at a Foundational Level?

The simplest place to begin is by clarifying the three mandatory capabilities required for any technology solution to enable a connected risk approach.

1. Connected Ecosystem

The technology solution must constitute a genuinely connected ecosystem that ties together the content and activities of your audit, risk, compliance, and InfoSec programs, including their data, analytics, controls, frameworks, and workflows. Every module must work together and share data.

2. Unified Data Core

The solution must create a unified data core that constitutes a single source of truth for the organization's risks, controls, issues, policies, and related information. This platform is where teams build and govern a single risk language via a single data architecture.

As alluded to earlier, this element also provides the foundations for effectively leveraging AI-powered analytics and insights. AI is predicated on clean, unified data; if you're running an AI program and it can only see across part of your data, it's not seeing—or presenting—the full picture of what your data is showing.

3. Core Task Automation and AI Integration

The technology should help to meaningfully reduce your organization's administrative burden.

Any truly modern technology platform should embed at least some automation of core tasks, helping to free up resources' valuable time. The more we can automate our core tasks in ways that make sense, the more we enable professionals across the three lines to focus on what truly matters and increase their impact on the business.

In the context of connected risk, core task automation should ideally address tasks and workflows such as data and evidence collection and reuse, testing activities, issue or risk authoring, report generation, and risk monitoring. With all that said, it's also important to ensure that automated solutions are built for purpose, such that the technology understands and easily integrates with users' day-to-day workflows. AI is critical in supporting these capabilities, given its ability to leverage purpose-built algorithms and other AI-powered technologies (e.g., generative AI, natural language processing, machine learning) to inform and streamline core task automation.

What Other Capabilities Can Connected Risk Technology Include?

The relentless advance of technology obviously prevents me from imagining 100 percent of the capabilities that connected risk technologies may ultimately offer. It's nevertheless helpful to understand some of the "bonus" capabilities that already exist or are likely to be developed. While solutions are not required to have these capabilities to enable a connected risk approach, considering these capabilities may be helpful as your organization determines which characteristics to seek in its enabling technologies.

Proactive and Predictive Insights

Making more forward-looking, risk-informed business decisions requires leveraging real-time risk data to drive proactive and predictive insights about potential issues, threats, and opportunities. For example, these capabilities may help organizations identify risks and issues that may be connected, detect areas of duplication, analyze ROI, or flag anomalies in the data, ineffective controls, coverage gaps, or potential areas of noncompliance.

Tools for Improving First-Line Engagement

Optimizing risk management requires effective first-line engagement, full stop. That's why "first-line engagement" is one of the key internal forces represented in the Connected Risk Model. Connected risk technology can provide first-line stakeholders with a single intuitive interface that helps them visualize risks and insights, make decisions, and take action as needed. This is a radical departure from the days of duplicative requests and misaligned reporting from different teams through multiple channels.

For example, connected risk technology can make the process of responding to questionnaires consistent and streamlined, regardless of where requests originate (e.g., risk assessment, IT audit, compliance exercise). It should be simple and intuitive to proactively report incidents or new emerging risks. When the first line is empowered to take a more active role in day-to-day risk management, overall risk management becomes exponentially stronger.

Personalized Workspaces

Everyone has their own needs and preferences when it comes to using technology. Workspaces and dashboards can be customized at the individual level, displaying the data and detail levels different stakeholders need in their roles. Each user is able to configure their notifications, updates, tasks, data displays, and any external integrations to fit their unique preferences.

Continuous Monitoring

True continuous monitoring—something of a "holy grail" for risk management—becomes increasingly attainable through connected risk technologies. Data and KRIs can be automatically scanned and analyzed behind the scenes to continuously identify and surface risks, issues, trends, patterns, and irregularities. For example, these capabilities could help organizations detect potential cybersecurity threats, breaches, and impacts; detect patterns of over- or under-testing of key controls; detect fraud; use horizon scanning and monitoring for regulatory and legislative activity (providing early warning of emerging compliance risks); monitor current regulatory compliance obligations to identify potential gaps and issues; and uncover opportunities for improving processes and workflows.

AI-Powered Recommendations

While a degree of AI is explicit or implied in many of the use cases mentioned earlier, AI's potential can manifest in countless ways within connected risk technology. Purpose-built AI capabilities may identify duplicate evidence requests or identify evidence already collected; suggest control mappings; connect issues raised by different functions; make recommendations in the context of a user's workflow; suggest data visualizations to convey key concepts; and expedite authoring of reports, issues, and risks.

Of course, human insight, judgment, creativity, and experience—along with human understanding of nuance, context, and the organization's risk strategy, priorities, and values—are the necessary layer required to translate

AI's recommendations into actionable guidance that informs better business decisions. AI's potential to provide intelligent recommendations that can help organizations understand where to focus, what actions to consider, and where action may be needed is nonetheless hugely promising.

Ability to Interface with Internal and External Partners

As compliance requirements for ESG, cybersecurity, data privacy, and other areas continue to grow in scope and complexity, having a reliable, secure, and consistent process for communicating requirements and sharing data with partners, vendors, suppliers, customers, and other third parties becomes increasingly crucial. It's not difficult to imagine how connected risk technologies could be expanded to support these capabilities.

Flexible Permissioning

Organizations establish permissions and oversight around segregation of duties (SoD) to help them manage the risks of someone accidentally or intentionally bypassing management's controls or misusing the organization's assets. Teams need to configure permissions to data and inputs with precision to engage connected risk stakeholders from the first line to the boardroom at the appropriate level of visibility and detail. If organizations are unable to give access across multiple teams and roles at the right levels, stakeholders may lack access to data they need or have more access than would be desired—potentially exposing sensitive data or sharing distracting data not relevant to their duties.

What ISN'T Connected Risk Technology?

Many legacy and modern tools may pitch you something that sounds an awful lot like connected risk, trumpeting a single, shared data set and shared technology. Unfortunately, these tools sometimes lack the capabilities that are essential to making connected risk work for your organization. Most often, they suffer from one or more of the following challenges:

- **Function-specific implementation.** The way many of these tools are implemented and customized by users still ultimately results in data siloing.

- **Too narrow a lens on connectivity.** The "connected risk" vision may be too narrowly focused on the needs and perspectives of one or more functional silos (e.g., CISOs, internal audit) or present bolt-on technology as if it were a unified platform. While these solutions may achieve connectivity from one or more specific perspectives in the organization, they lack true cross-organizational connectivity.
- **Poor user experience.** Teams are unable to use the technology on a day-to-day basis to capture data in a structured, real-time manner. Again, if teams are resistant to using the technology, how likely is its implementation to change the game for the better?
- **Retroactive reports, not proactive insights.** Dashboards and data views are more focused on reporting lagging indicators than on identifying proactive insights (e.g., leading indicators, gaps) needed to inform discussions and decision-making at the management and board levels.

What Does Connected Risk Look Like for You?

You can't choose the right technology for your needs until you determine, in collaboration with others, what connected risk itself looks like for your organization. While we can glean some ideas from looking at general trends, solutions will vary from organization to organization. Accordingly, before you can initiate genuinely productive conversations about technology selection and implementation, it's necessary to gain an understanding of what needs to be connected.

To that end, start by talking with the various second- and third-line leaders in your organization. After all, communication is fundamental to connected risk. The conversations should focus on what "connected risk" looks like for their department: What are the data needs for each role? As in, what specific data points need to be connected? What current-state technology limitations are preventing them from doing their jobs more effectively?

You're likely to find commonalities and themes across the different teams—which then become excellent choices for getting started with connected risk. For example:

- **Shared issue tracking** tends to be a top request across risk management, InfoSec, compliance, and internal audit teams.
- Risk management teams generally seek to ensure that **other teams' work supports their assessment and prioritization of risks** (e.g., residual risk inputs, insights from other teams' risk assessments), and to **consolidate risk mitigation and issue remediation workflows**.
- Compliance teams often look to **share risk assessments and controls** and **gain internal audit's assurance over reporting metrics** (e.g., ESG data assurance is an increasingly common request).
- Internal audit is often focused on **using a unified risk and control matrix** to help them identify, rank, and implement controls used to mitigate risks, and on ensuring that **enterprise risks are directly tied to audit planning**.
- InfoSec teams also tend to seek **shared visibility and reporting** on risk areas across the organization, as well as the **ability to leverage other teams' risk insights** to ensure security efforts are focused on the most important risks. They also want to improve their understanding of **how technology risks impact enterprise risks**.
- Many second- and third-line teams are interested in **consolidating reporting** to executive management and the board.

These are the types of requests that tend to be top-of-mind for most teams. As your organization's key risk players better understand potential capabilities, they're likely to refine and add to their initial requests. Once their requirements take shape, you'll want to seek out technology that supports the specific needs outlined.

Of course, connected risk isn't solely focused on serving second- and third-line teams: it is designed to support and engage stakeholders across the organization. That said, because second- and third-line functions' activities are responsible for assurance on the overall effectiveness of risk management, it's the right place to start in understanding your technology needs.

In the end, your connected risk technology solution should help you improve business outcomes, including faster identification and resolution of risks and issues, simpler prioritization, increased team productivity, more effective decision-making, and stronger partnerships across the three lines. Remember, connected risk thinking focuses on outcomes, not outputs. Choose the solution that will best support your organization in making decisions, taking action, and achieving results.

Technology Is Foundational for Connected Risk

The bottom line is that communication, coordination, context, and collaboration without technology are suboptimal. Any organization planning to remain relevant and resilient in the uncertain future ahead must make the right technology investments today. After all, investing in technology that's ill-matched to your organization's needs can be a competitive advantage—for your competitors.

Technology, used to strategically augment the great minds and ideas that give your organization a reason for existing, is the tool we use to expand what's possible. As Amazon founder Jeff Bezos said, "In today's era of volatility, there is no other way but to reinvent. The only sustainable advantage you can have over others is agility, that's it. Because nothing else is sustainable, everything else you create, somebody else will replicate."

CHAPTER 12

The "Wow Factor" from Connected Risk Alignment

Connected risk agents of change must learn how to speak compellingly about the value of connected risk with others in the organization.

This requires painting a vision of the future. Permacrisis has challenged boards and C-suite leaders like never before. They want to know how to identify emerging risks, how to decide when risks need attention or mitigation, and how to take action. (The most common response when I ask audit committee members what they most need from internal audit is "no surprises.") In other words, they want foresight—the ability to contemplate the key risks and challenges their organizations could conceivably face. They want the ability to prepare for challenges before they materialize and avoid the disasters and missed opportunities that have occasioned the demise of so many organizations during the first half of the 2020s. In short, they want a crystal ball.

I am writing this book because I am confident that connected risk is the best equivalent to a crystal ball that we have available. Teams operating at a high level of connected risk maturity are more confident in their ability to help management and the board know where to look, what to prioritize, where to turn, and how to take action. They are best equipped to help their organizations avoid surprises.

I will always remember the first time I pointed out an emerging risk during the course of an internal audit. My client sat up straighter as his eyes widened. Then he said, "Oh, I hadn't thought of that." That moment felt deeply rewarding because I knew my work was having an impact.

At the end of the day, every professional across all three lines wants to have an impact and provide value. For audit, risk, compliance, and InfoSec teams in particular, the stakes around risk management are higher because the pinnacle of success in these roles is the ability to serve as strategic partners to the business. In many organizations, these teams haven't felt that way. They see limitations—not potential.

Connected risk reduces or removes these limitations to help teams realize their potential. It ties together all of their strengths, activating them as superpowers. Whereas nobody has yet unearthed a truly credible crystal ball, perhaps the enhanced, empowered risk management approach enabled by connected risk can help us develop the audit, risk, compliance, and InfoSec equivalents of X-ray vision, superhuman senses, and clairvoyance we need to approximate one within the world of business.

There is a very real "wow" factor associated with connected risk and connected risk technologies. I'm convinced—sufficiently impressed to devote an entire book to extolling its necessity for the modern age. Most likely, however, people in your organization will need convincing. This chapter exists to help you make the case for implementing connected risk in your organization, demonstrate and evangelize its potential and value, and identify and cultivate champions across all three lines. Invisible superhero cape strongly implied.

Perfect Your Connected Risk Elevator Pitch

We're all familiar with the "elevator pitch," which strives to capture the essence of a value proposition in the time it takes to ride an elevator (60 seconds or less). While your exact connected risk elevator pitch will vary based on the risks facing your organization and your role within it, the following is a starting point.

Our stakeholders need us to protect and create value, but risks are emerging and changing faster than ever and we have limited resources for responding. We're not maximizing the benefit of our risk resources and data, which means we could be missing risks—and missing opportunities. We can fix this by better connecting our teams, risk data, and processes across functions using purpose-built technology, intelligent automation, and a unified control architecture and data core. This approach is called "connected risk," and it can help us see and respond to risks in real time, improve how internal and external stakeholders work together, increase risk awareness and ownership across the organization, and get ahead of the risks our competitors may not see.

The best elevator pitches, of course, are custom-tailored to their audience, speaking to their specific pain points and priorities. For example:

- If you're talking to someone on the **ERM** team, share how connected risk will help them achieve a higher level of risk management for their organization. Many CROs and ERM leaders feel that resource constraints (or the limitations of their own experience) prevent them from being as effective as possible. Connected risk helps them harness the collective power of the key risk players to up their game (e.g., centralized issue tracking prioritizing high-impact issues, increased visibility into how issues impact one another).
- If you're talking to **internal audit**, tell them about the unified risk and control matrix that will help them eliminate duplicative testing and place more reliance on the work of other risk teams. Emphasize how connected risk can help drive conformance with The IIA's *Standards* and allocate resources to risk areas of higher importance to the organization, helping to ensure that internal audit remains relevant, aligned with organizational strategy, and focused on value.
- If you're talking with someone in **InfoSec**, explain how connected risk will make it easier to create awareness of key data protection responsibilities and controls, as well as provide a higher level of assurance that key data will be protected and cybersecurity threats will be thwarted. For example, InfoSec teams can use connected risk AI tools to automatically analyze data across the enterprise, scan applications and systems for threats and vulnerabilities, automate routine tasks (e.g., compliance checks, security), and assess risk likelihood and impact, enabling more effective prioritization.
- If you've finally got the **CEO or CFO**'s attention, explain how connected risk can help save costs and improve resource allocation by:

    - ▹ Eliminating duplicative work being performed by multiple parties

- Consolidating processes and technologies in ways that reduce costs
- Preventing unnecessary costs from impacts of negative or disaster events, drawing either from your own loss data or relevant benchmarking data from other companies
- Aligning insights and reporting from second- and third-line teams, helping to eliminate conflicting viewpoints and support them in making more effective risk-based decisions
- Enabling more effective leverage of AI technologies to drive value from the organization's data

However you construct your pitch, here is the core of what it needs to communicate: risk has changed, so risk management must follow suit. The siloed teams, resource constraints, labor-intensive processes, and disconnected data and legacy technologies plaguing most organizations are preventing them from making the most of their limited risk resources. Going forward, organizations need to take a deliberate, transformative approach to improving collaboration, communication, and connection across teams, data, and processes to enable them to surface better insights that risk resources can translate to better foresight. As I wrote in a 2023 Forbes article (again displaying my well-known appreciation of a timely metaphor):

> Today's unpredictable riptides of risk require all hands on deck, everyone rowing in the same direction and near-constant scanning of the horizon for both expected and unexpected risks...We're not out of the risk management riptides yet. The volatile risk environment that has so far characterized the 2020s is not abating, and we are all still trying to break free. Externally produced resources, heeded alongside internal resources that can help you understand how well you're managing risk, are lifelines you ignore at your peril. Make the most of the resources you have at your fingertips, both within and outside of your organization. Only through risk management can you protect, grow and enhance the value you're entrusted with by your shareholders.[1]

There is absolutely a heightened sense of urgency among business leaders and boards to find new and better routes to safety and success. They want answers and they need ideas, so they are likely to hear you out—especially if simply making better use of existing resources is central to your proposed solution. If your elevator ride with that C-suite executive or board member is only to the next floor down, get their attention with your version of the absolute bottom-line message of connected risk: together, "we" are stronger than "me."

Build and Tailor Your Business Case

Once you get your foot in the door, you'll need plenty of ready-to-deploy arguments to demonstrate how connected risk can solve pain points while protecting, realizing, and creating value across the business. Thankfully, connected risk promises big outcomes and benefits that most professionals will readily comprehend. While the following descriptions reiterate many of the benefits mentioned earlier, I have rephrased them here in plain language that hones in on key context.

Connected, Strategic View of Risk

Dynamic data collection provides your organization with a unified data core and "single source of truth." Because all teams are working from the same pool of data (often sharing testing and assessment results), they have increased visibility on risks and reporting across the organization—as well as a clear view of how different risks interconnect and enable achievement of the overall strategy. This more strategic view on risk informs more effective audit and assessment planning, prioritization of risks and issues, and risk-based decision-making. Instead of the sprawling risk register of years past, your organization is equipped with a smaller set of prioritized risks that are tied to strategy via coherent narratives. This enables more targeted outcome-based thinking and approaches based on an enhanced understanding of where risk management efforts will have more impact.

What they need to understand: In years past, looking at the organization's top 10 to 40 risks was often sufficient. Such a limited view has become laughable in permacrisis. The average organization's risk universe now grows exponentially each year, given the domino effect created by the interrelated nature of risk. Organizations need visibility on how risks in one area roll up to others. This is a central challenge driving the connected risk mandate forward.

Data-Driven Insights

A connected risk approach helps to drive more value from your organization's data, efficiently surfacing issues and insights that may otherwise go unnoticed. These AI-enabled insights help increase front-line engagement while enabling all three lines to direct efforts to higher-impact areas. Insights can also be mined to validate investments, promote more risk-aware decisions, highlight opportunities, and more.

What they need to understand: Simply having data doesn't translate to driving value from data. People often assume their organizations are already actively leveraging their data to better grasp the organizations' most pressing risks and compelling opportunities. Sadly, disconnected data can yield only so much value, and your second- and third-line teams' insights are only as good as the data upon which they're built.

Faster Risk Detection and Issue Resolution

Because teams are now sharing insights, data, assessments, testing results, and issue tracking, they can more quickly identify risks, issues, and opportunities—and work together to create a single action plan focused on mitigating the risk, resolving the issue, or realizing the opportunity. As a result, first-line teams are able to act more quickly on insights to resolve issues, all while operating with greater confidence, trust, and assurance.

What they need to understand: Without a connected risk approach, different risk teams often track—and work on multiple separate solutions to—the same issues. They are duplicating efforts when they could band together to enact a faster, more powerful solution.

Increased Agility

So much of effective risk management and resilience in permacrisis boils down to becoming more agile in how we respond to emerging and changing threats and opportunities. Connected risk helps every team in your organization to increase its agility. Existing audit plans can easily be tweaked to reflect a new risk that has emerged. A newly surfaced insight can trigger more focus in one area or a reduction in another. Teams are able to adapt and pivot as needed, becoming more nimble in ways that better serve overall business goals. In a connected risk environment, people tend to be less focused on "checking boxes" and more focused on dynamic planning that flexes to serve the business's overall objectives.

What they need to understand: So much of historical risk management boils down to lists: lists of risks, lists of audits, lists of tasks, lists of issues. This often engenders a rigid approach to planning and execution wherein an audit gets done simply because it's on the plan—not because the team has validated that the audit is still called for given existing risk conditions.

Intuitive, Purpose-Built Technology People Want to Use

True connected risk technology has been purpose-built to integrate with the day-to-day workflows of a wide range of users. It is simple and intuitive to use, making onboarding easy and adoption a no-brainer. It's also customizable, with dashboards that can be dialed in to display and compare organizational data to fit each user's needs.

When done right, AI-enabled connected risk technology makes it easy to identify and reuse evidence, find and connect risk or control issues, document new issues or controls (leveraging existing ones to expedite drafting), automate repetitive tasks, and access research that helps teams expedite tasks or leverage work that has been completed. In other words, connected risk technology is designed to make risk management simpler, more efficient, more engaging, and ultimately more rewarding. This is a non-negligible benefit in any organization's quest to attract and retain top talent.

What they need to understand: Technology solutions must be able to address stakeholder needs at many levels of the organization, meeting the everyday needs of a multitude of everyday users. There's the person charged with collecting evidence. There's the person testing the controls, and the one charged to create new risks in the system. There's the person managing open issues. There's also the person at the director or manager level who needs to quickly understand what everything means for the decisions they need to make. The technology you choose must work for all of these stakeholders in a way that makes sense for their needs and workflows. If it doesn't, requiring users to relearn how to do their work, they will resist using it—and it won't create the value you seek.

Unified Control Architecture

A unified risk and control matrix brings together all of your organization's controls, using a shared taxonomy and a single set of definitions. Everyone is speaking the same language, and process definitions and responsibilities are clear and consistent across the organization, enabling democratized ownership of controls. Because there are no duplicative controls, there's also no duplicative testing. Control gaps and issues are easier to identify and more clear-cut to remediate. Teams have increased visibility on the overall effectiveness of controls and a more granular view of coverage.

What they need to understand: A unified control architecture allows organizations to distribute controls ownership much more effectively. Without one, you may have eight different process definitions and just as many disparate taxonomies, making it difficult for control owners to understand what they're responsible for. It's also much harder to identify gaps in controls and coverage.

Saved Time and Effort That Can Be Redirected

I've touched several times on the obvious value of reducing duplication of effort and audit fatigue. A connected risk approach also reduces the overall burden on the business. As mundane or repetitive tasks are automated or handled by AI, teams are able to invest more of their time in higher-value work. They're spending less time on rote analysis, and more time applying judgment and creativity to that analysis to understand context and uncover what's really important.

What they need to understand: Without technology, human workers can't possibly see and monitor the full picture of, and interconnections between, the organization's risks. AI, automation, machine learning, process mining, and other technologies are the capacity multipliers and strategic accelerants organizations need to keep pace with the speed of risk.

Risk Management Culture Embedded across the Organization

Customized dashboards displaying real-time risk data and insights bring risk into focus and make day-to-day risk management accessible to all. With a better understanding of how risk impacts their role and work, the entire organization is more engaged, educated, and empowered to have an impact. This is the cultural shift organizations need to transform risk management.

What they need to understand: The ultimate purpose of risk management is to enable organizational success. That requires embedding risk management at every level of the organization, such that every employee and every stakeholder understands—and is invested in—the importance of monitoring and managing risk. This overarching objective rose to the surface as our understanding of risk management grew, as seen in the evolution of COSO’s ERM framework, ISO 31000’s risk management guidelines, and The IIA’s Three Lines Model.

Increased Ability to Drive Competitive Advantage

Organizations that achieve high maturity in their connected risk approaches are better positioned to drive competitive advantage. While it is still no crystal ball, it is an undoubtedly powerful tool that empowers stakeholders at every level to increase their impact. The manager on the front line in the factory has the right information at the right detail level to help them focus on staying ahead of what’s next. The C-suite executive knows which risks they’ll focus on at the next board meeting.

What they need to understand: There is no escaping permacrisis. We can, however, make changes that shift how we use resources and improve how we communicate, collaborate, and capitalize on each of our strengths. The organizations that remain resilient and relevant in permacrisis will have taken action to make the most of the valuable resources they already possess.

Show Them What They’ll Be Missing

Focusing on the benefits is not, of course, sufficient for convincing every audience. Some stakeholders need to feel the “fear of missing out” to find their motivation.

In these cases, consider highlighting the consequences of *not* implementing connected risk. Be willing to highlight the myriad competitors and leading companies embracing connected risk. These consequences are essentially the flip sides of all the right reasons to adopt a connected risk approach. I outlined these impacts in chapter 6 in the section entitled “How the Gap Impacts Organizations,” which should offer plenty of fuel to inspire the desired levels of fear.

Getting on the Path

Connected risk will be a journey that looks different for every organization. No organization can do it all at once. Once you've surmounted the initial challenges of convincing your organization to get on the path and completing a few foundational projects, it's time to focus on futureproofing your connected risk strategy.

Risk will keep changing. Fortunately, connected risk will help you stay flexible and nimble to better meet its demands—but the journey is never over, so it's imperative to set a course for increasing maturity. In the next section, I'll offer knowledge and resources to help your organization make the most of connected risk's promise.

Part 5

Futureproofing for Risk Resilience

CHAPTER 13

Continuous Risk Monitoring

To achieve their objectives, organizations must be able to adapt to changing conditions. Accordingly, they must have a mechanism for getting the real-time information they need to adapt appropriately.

This may not sound revolutionary, but it marks a significant change in risk management strategy for most organizations, which have historically assessed risks periodically. In many cases, risk assessments and audit plans are updated annually (or quarterly at best), providing only point-in-time snapshots of risk management effectiveness and minimal or no access to real-time information and insights.

It's not difficult to see the problem: if you ran a warehouse operation, would you limit security camera surveillance to taking only one picture per day to determine whether there is an intruder outside of your door? Obviously not, because 23 hours and 59 seconds thereby remain unaccounted for—and even if your single photo did manage to capture a theft in progress, you won't know about it until the thief is long gone.

Effective risk management in the era of permacrisis requires basing efforts on continuous assessment of risks and up-to-date information—the equivalent of multiple security cameras running 24/7, the footage of which is being monitored for unusual activity in real time. In this way, organizations can get the information they need to adapt risk focus areas, coverage, audit plans, and action plans at a pace commensurate with the speed of risk. This is the imperative for continuous risk monitoring.

The lamentable reality is that true continuous risk monitoring is not widely practiced. Where it is happening, it often relies on homegrown systems that lack sophistication and connection with overall risk management and strategy. Further, many organizations that claim to continuously monitor risk are in fact only performing assessments every two or three months. That's not continuous, and that's not what's needed.

Why isn't continuous risk monitoring happening in more organizations? Most are simply intimidated and lacking in experience, unsure how to do it or where to begin. In some cases, management is hesitant to invest. It is nevertheless a key risk management and audit responsibility and a critical competency to cultivate in today's volatile risk environment. It is also a central tenet of connected risk.

The good news is that continuous risk monitoring isn't as challenging or resource-intensive as many assume. This chapter shares proven strategies and practical tactics for getting started.

Defining Continuous Risk Monitoring

Continuous risk monitoring is an ongoing process that enables organizations to identify, assess, and manage risks and impacts in real time. It is used in conjunction with periodic risk assessments to enable organizations to assess how risk levels are changing—as well as how controls are performing—over time. As a result, instead of relying solely on the infrequent, point-in-time snapshots provided by traditional approaches, organizations also have real-time awareness and reporting of threats, vulnerabilities, and opportunities. This mix enables more effective decision-making and faster responses to mitigate threats, address vulnerabilities before they cause problems, capitalize on opportunities, and limit the organization's risks to acceptable levels. Indeed, a continuous approach provides a more reliable assessment of risks relative to risk appetites and strategies, enabling organizations to more effectively set priorities and thresholds and manage risk accordingly.

Professional standards and guidance for internal auditors and risk managers reinforce the need for a continuous approach, outlining principles and basic components. They do not, however, provide specific guidance regarding implementation. For example:

- One of the five foundational components of **COSO's ERM framework, "Information, Communication, and Reporting,"** stipulates that ERM "requires a continual process of obtaining and sharing necessary information, from both internal and external sources, which flows up, down, and across the organization."[1]

- The IIA's *Standards* require internal auditors to conduct an organization-wide risk assessment at least annually to form the basis for their audit plans. The "Considerations for Implementation" for **Standard 9.4 Internal Audit Plan** continue, "However, the chief audit executive should keep continuously apprised of risk information, updating the risk assessment and internal audit plan accordingly" and later, "The chief audit executive may implement a methodology for continuously assessing risks."[2]

That said, InfoSec professionals are notably ahead of the game on how-to guidance. For example, ISACA's COBIT 5, issued in 2012, provides a comprehensive, principles-based framework for defining continuous risk monitoring governance and processes. The U.S. Department of Commerce National Institute of Standards and Technology's (NIST's) Special Publication 800-137 (NIST SP 800-137), *Information Security Continuous Monitoring (ISCM) for Federal Information Systems and Organizations*, published in 2011, also offers detailed guidance for information security continuous monitoring, defined as "maintaining ongoing awareness of information security, vulnerabilities, and threats to support organizational risk management decisions."[3]

While NIST SP 800-137 was written to address the needs of InfoSec professionals, many of its lessons seem equally resonant across all of continuous risk monitoring. Consider the following, which aptly summarizes what's at stake in the face of the growing risk exposure gap.

> Ongoing monitoring is a critical part of [the] risk management process... to ensure that organization-wide operations remain within an acceptable level of risk, despite any changes that occur. Timely, relevant, and accurate information is vital, particularly when resources are limited and agencies must prioritize their efforts.[4]

The Growing Importance of Continuous Risk Monitoring

Continuous risk monitoring, long seen as a leading practice, is quickly becoming a strategic business imperative. It is mission-critical not only for connected risk, but also for enabling the agility, resilience, and strategic focus demanded by permacrisis. After all, how likely are we to avoid surprises and effectively pivot if we insist exclusively on conducting audits and assessments the traditional way, based on plans that are six months to a year old?

The answer is obvious. The only viable path forward is to enable our organizations to assess risk on a continual basis, giving us the fresh information needed to adapt risk management in real time.

What's more, continuous risk monitoring is becoming increasingly critical for complying with regulatory requirements. For example:

- As mentioned in chapter 4, the SEC's cybersecurity rule mandates that public companies continuously monitor for cyber incidents and materiality to comply with the rule's immediate reporting requirements, which require disclosure of material incidents via Form 8-K within four business days.[5] Within this time frame, companies must not only detect the incident within their systems, but also assess its materiality, prepare the required disclosure, and file it with the SEC. Most organizations' monitoring capabilities will be challenged by these tight turnarounds.
- The SEC's climate disclosure rules require public companies to provide certain climate-related risk information both within and outside their financial statements. Because the requirements necessitate understanding the actual or likely material impacts of climate-related risks on business strategy, results of operations, financial condition, business model, and outlook, the ability to continuously track and monitor these risks and impacts becomes vital.[6]

Leading internal auditors recognize the growing criticality of a continuous approach. When asked to identify which area most contributes to making an internal audit function relevant, nearly one in five CAEs in Protiviti's *2023 Next Generation Internal Audit Survey* pinpoint "embracing continuous monitoring to accelerate reporting and reflect business changes."[7] In the IAF's 2024 *Risk in Focus—North America*, Harold Silverman, The IIA's senior director of CAE and corporate governance engagement, echoes this priority.

> CAEs must be clued into organizational strategies, which means not conducting static risk assessments nor having an event-based audit plan that is inflexible...Emerging technologies [and] market changes are dynamic risk events in themselves so CAEs must constantly be alert to re-evaluate what they are auditing and how.[8]

Benefits of Continuous Risk Monitoring

The overall value proposition of continuous risk monitoring—providing the real-time information organizations need to adapt appropriately to changing conditions—should be readily evident to most stakeholders. The following points may prove beneficial if you need help spelling it out.

By developing effective strategies for continuously monitoring risk, organizations also enable:

- **Timely detection of threats, vulnerabilities, and opportunities, supporting faster responses.** Early detection of potential risks and issues can save organizations considerable time, money, and headaches while providing valuable insights on ways the organization can better protect itself going forward. Technology-enabled monitoring can analyze the entire monitored environment in real time—not just by reviewing samples after the fact.
- **Enhanced decision-making based on more accurate, timely information focused on the risks that matter most.** Internal audit, risk, compliance, and InfoSec teams step up as trusted advisors able to share relevant, transparent risk reporting, guidance, and insights. Key first-line stakeholders can embrace a self-service model to access data, KRIs, and insights impacting their work. Technology enablement can further improve trust and transparency in reporting by removing a degree of human subjectivity and error.
- **Increased adaptability, agility, and resilience.** The organization has an enhanced ability to assess relevant data and KPIs, surface

potential issues and data-enabled insights, and pivot when needed, as well as proactively manage risk tolerance to acceptable levels.

- **Resource optimization that frees up resources to focus on higher-value work.** Technology enablement automates certain aspects of monitoring and reporting, reducing the time, cost, and effort required for ongoing risk management. This enables second- and third-line teams to focus their time on more critical risks while allowing the organization to address *more* risks overall. It also reduces the stakeholder audit fatigue common in traditional approaches.
- **Improved ability to meet compliance and regulatory requirements.** As mentioned, many organizations face new regulations requiring timely issue identification and disclosures and ongoing monitoring of key metrics. Technology-enabled continuous risk monitoring can support faster identification, ongoing tracking, and streamlined review and reporting.
- **More timely assurance on the effectiveness of risk management.** Continuously monitoring risks can enhance internal audit's agility, enabling more flexible and dynamic audit planning. A lack of continuous risk monitoring resulted in swiftly outdated internal audit plans during the onset of COVID-19 in 2020, and the onset of geopolitical conflicts in early 2022 and late 2023.

Guiding Principles for Continuous Risk Monitoring

Every organization has different risk management needs, priorities, and appetites. That said, the following four principles can help guide any organization's approach to continuous risk monitoring.

1. Recognize Risk Volatility and Velocity

Make sure you're assessing risk across all dimensions. While likelihood and impact remain key factors in the overall risk rating, velocity and volatility should also be considered. Chapter 3 takes a more detailed look at risk velocity and volatility.

2. Deploy Efficient and Effective Continuous Monitoring Strategies

The core need is to deploy a system of mechanisms by which your organization can periodically check in on and be alerted to change, dissipation, or emergence of key risks. The following pages discuss several options that your organization can consider. Organizations should use multiple strategies in tandem.

3. Understand That Technology Is an Integral Part of Continuous Risk Monitoring

Humans simply cannot monitor risk 24/7 without technology's help. This truth is reflected in medical technologies that monitor patient health. Warning and recording devices detect changes or patterns in patients' vital functions. Other devices carefully measure out doses of anesthesia, pain management, or other medications. These devices and practices were developed based on evidence consistently showing that "our human senses by themselves, are not reliable in keeping 'eternal vigilance'," as "Monitoring the Monitors—Beyond Risk Management," describes the problem.[9]

All this to say, true continuous risk monitoring requires technology enablement. Technology-based automation supports real-time visibility into risks across the organization, gathering data, tracking KRIs, identifying trends and deviations, creating customized, streamlined reporting and data visualizations, and more. The key is achieving the balance of technology enablement and human analysis and decision-making that is appropriate for your strategy and risk appetite. Again, NIST SP 800-137 offers sound advice.

> Organization-wide monitoring cannot be efficiently achieved through manual processes alone or through automated processes alone. Where manual processes are used, the processes are repeatable and verifiable to enable consistent implementation. Automated processes, including the use of automated support tools (e.g., vulnerability scanning tools, network scanning devices), can make the process of continuous monitoring more cost-effective, consistent, and efficient.[10]

The rapid emergence of AI also offers the promise of improved continuous risk monitoring capabilities. Depending on the KRIs or other continuous monitoring strategies deployed, AI can assist with automated data analysis, predictive analytics, risk scoring, and compliance monitoring. It can also be deployed to provide real-time alerts when key metrics signal that risks are shifting.

4. Maintain a 360-Degree View

As I have stressed, effective risk management in permacrisis requires constantly scanning the horizon in all directions. This means looking not only for the risks already visible, but also striving to imagine and predict those on and beyond the horizon. You will do this more successfully if you:

- **Ensure collaboration across all three lines, planning and executing in coordination and ongoing communication.** This is the very essence of connected risk. The more sets of eyes you have looking out at the horizon, the greater the likelihood that your organization will be able to identify and stay focused on its key risks.
- **Validate that your continuous risk monitoring strategy addresses the needs of all relevant stakeholders.** Invest time early in identifying and understanding key needs, priorities, concerns, and potential roadblocks. Reevaluate periodically to ensure ongoing coverage and fit.
- **Regularly communicate with management and the board.** An effective continuous risk monitoring strategy is—to again quote NIST SP 800-137—"grounded in a clear understanding of organizational risk tolerance [helping] officials set priorities and manage risk consistently throughout the organization."[11] Avoiding surprises in this area necessitates ongoing communication with the audit committee, board, and management to ensure that the strategy remains aligned with the organization's risk appetite and priorities.

Strategies for Continuous Risk Monitoring

AuditBoard's *2023 Focus on the Future* survey asked internal audit leaders to identify the methods they use for continuously monitoring risks. The data reflected that:

- Most respondents talk with other risk and assurance functions (86 percent) and business management (74 percent) to expand and deepen their understanding of the organization's risks.
- A majority (72 percent) also proactively monitor sector changes and trends.
- A little more than half (52 percent) monitor KRIs.
- Only half report engaging with other internal auditors, and less than half (46 percent) review the types of third-party reports and surveys we referenced in chapter 4.[12]

While these results show that many organizations are making concerted efforts toward continuous risk monitoring, true risk management effectiveness requires using more of the continuous monitoring methods at our disposal. For example, talking with other risk and assurance leaders and reviewing external reports and surveys are highly advantageous strategies requiring relatively little outlay of effort—and yet, about half of the polled respondents failed to capitalize on either method.

The right answer for your organization is likely to combine several of the following common strategies. Each method is more powerful when integrated into technology solutions and used in conjunction with other continuous monitoring approaches.

Key Risk Indicators (KRIs)

Whereas key performance indicators (KPIs) alert organizations to risk events that have already impacted the organization, KRIs help identify potential shifts in risk conditions that may impact the organization in the future.

Think of KRIs as an early warning risk detection system. By providing visibility into potential weaknesses in the organization's risk/control environment and processes, KRIs help to surface potential risks that could impact the business.

A COSO publication titled *Developing Key Risk Indicators to Strengthen Enterprise Risk Management* defines KRIs as metrics or indicators that help "better monitor potential future shifts in risk conditions or new emerging risks so that management and boards are able to more proactively identify potential impacts to the organization's portfolio of risks."[13] Indeed, KRIs enable organizations to quantify, assess, monitor, and sometimes benchmark different types of risk events. This allows for more timely assurance on the effectiveness of risk management and more expedient, strategic, and proactive development of risk mitigation approaches and overall risk strategy. KRIs also help establish increased objectivity in the risk management process.

Characteristics and Examples

KRIs can be qualitative, using probabilities to predict potential outcomes, or quantitative, based on numerical data and verifiable facts based on analyses, models, and other outputs. The types of KRIs that are most relevant for your organization depend on the nature of your business, industry, strategy, priorities, and other internal (e.g., lack of first-line engagement, outdated technologies) and external factors (e.g., third-party risk, environmental impacts). To provide value, all KRIs should be measurable, comparable, predictable, and informational, helping to provide a clear and intuitive view of the risk highlighted.

The following are examples of KRIs in several categories.

- **Cybersecurity:** A spike in attempted cyber intrusions may indicate heightened risk of a data breach.
- **Human resources:** A sudden increase in staff turnover could signal a troubled culture or foreshadow staff shortages that could impact organizational performance and achievement of objectives.
- **Financial:** Economic forecasts indicating a slowing economy or recession could indicate a heightened risk of declining sales revenues in the year ahead.
- **Technological:** An increase in the frequency or duration of system outages may signal increased risk of potential disruptions to operations that could reduce productivity or profitability.
- **Operational:** High error rates in key processes may indicate a heightened risk of future operational disruption.
- **Compliance:** Low rates of completion on employee compliance training (e.g., workplace safety, data privacy/security, code of conduct) could signal increasing compliance risks or gaps.
- **Third-party:** Protracted delivery times, more frequent quality issues, or even increased negative mentions on social media could

signal increasing risk that a third-party relationship could negatively impact your organization's operations and reputation.

- **Sustainability:** Metrics such as energy consumption per unit of output, amount of waste generated per unit of output, and percentage of materials recycled can signal increased risks relative to an organization's sustainability performance.
- **Culture:** Rapid growth, layoffs, acquisitions, divestitures, reorganizations, or high attrition can all signal increased organizational culture risks.
- **Customer:** A spike in customer complaints may signal increased risks of product or service quality and future demand.

Organizations should use a mix of leading and lagging KRIs to gain a complete and accurate picture of risk management effectiveness.

Lagging KRIs are backward-looking metrics that help organizations assess what has already occurred in the business, focusing on factors later in the sequence of causation to confirm trends and determine whether targets have been achieved. These KRIs are important for evaluating past performance and identifying potential areas of improvement.

Examples of lagging KRIs include metrics such as staff training completions, debt-to-equity ratios, number of customer complaints, employee turnover rates, and so on.

Leading KRIs, on the other hand, are forward-looking metrics that help predict future outcomes by measuring factors earlier in the sequence of causation to assess whether targets are likely to be achieved. These KRIs provide organizations with data that can highlight potential issues or weaknesses before they become problems and enable proactive responses. These KRIs are particularly critical in supporting ongoing alignment between your organization's risk appetite and risk management efforts, given that they can warn you when conditions indicate that risks may be meeting or exceeding desired thresholds. They also support more informed predictions about future risk conditions and impacts.

Examples of leading KRIs include metrics such as the number of managers who have completed workplace safety training, the number of employees certified on how and when to use the ethics hotline, the number of monitoring tools and technologies set up to detect and prevent cyberattacks, and so on.

Process

On a day-to-day basis, management (e.g., the CRO or others) is ultimately responsible for continuously monitoring KRIs. Internal auditors and other key risk players can assist management in assessing and leveraging KRIs to surface potential risks, issues, and insights. Internal audit should also validate and provide assurance around the KRI process (including KRI relevance and suitability), and identify, document, and report exceptions or breaches to KRIs.

Because KRIs enable organizations to monitor risk-related events that may affect the achievement of objectives, selecting and designing KRIs should begin by aligning with organizational objectives. KRIs should be tailored to your risk profile, taking into account the major risks facing your organization and risk appetite. Because it's simply not practical to create, monitor, and analyze every possible relevant KRI, it's important to prioritize the most significant risks.

Stakeholders: KRI selection should involve relevant stakeholders across all three lines, including leaders from each business unit and internal audit, risk, compliance, and InfoSec team members. Ideally, the business unit leaders should identify KRIs, set thresholds, perform monitoring, and identify anomalies, and the second-and third-line teams should provide input.

How to get started: Start by analyzing risk events that have affected the organization in the past (or present). Working backward, pinpoint intermediate and root-cause events that led to the ultimate loss or missed opportunity. These become your KRIs.

Maintenance: Conduct regular periodic reviews (annually at minimum) of the validity of KRIs as conditions evolve. Revisit whether you are using the right KRIs or if changes in the control environment necessitate the development of new KRIs.

"Shoe Leather" Assessments, or "Risk Assessment by Walking Around"

This method of continuous risk monitoring is precisely what it sounds like: walking around and talking with other risk and assurance professionals and members of business and functional management. Of course, in remote teams, "walking around" may entail regular check-ins via video conferencing or messaging—in which case, it could be tagged "risk assessment by logging on."

While I typically talk about "shoe leather" assessments relative to internal audit, they can be a powerful way for professionals across all three lines to understand and monitor the shifting velocity, volatility, and direction of key risks.

"Shoe leather" assessments lack the formality of KRI monitoring. Nevertheless, they will always be a critical monitoring strategy for internal audit. Internal auditors may have a broader view on risks across the organization, but first- and second-line professionals are more likely to recognize emerging risks or perceive shifts in the likelihood, impact, or velocity of known risks. These conversations may reveal key emerging risks or changes to existing risks that your KRIs do not.

That said, let's be absolutely clear: "shoe leather" assessments are only valid as continuous risk monitoring if they are done with discipline, regularity, and a broad reach. Further, for the strategy to be effective, risk, audit, compliance, and InfoSec professionals should collaborate and focus on building strong working relationships with the individuals they've committed to speaking with regularly.

How to get started: Audit, risk, compliance, and InfoSec teams should collaboratively build a relationship map to formalize a comprehensive coverage plan. Whereas an organizational chart typically focuses on showing working and reporting relationships, a relationship map is a visual diagram highlighting key business entities and leaders and documenting relationships with first-line management and other team members. Your relationship map should allocate key relationships across the wider team. Establish a regular cadence for interactions, setting the expectation that conversations can be formal or informal.

Maintenance: Revisit the relationship map periodically (at least annually) to ensure adequate coverage of key business entities and stakeholders.

"Connecting the Dots" from Internal Audits

Audit committees, boards, executives, and first- and second-line teams often look to internal audit to help connect the dots to understand the organization's risks and the overall effectiveness of risk management. In the context of continuous risk monitoring, "connecting the dots" is a metaphor for bringing the big picture of risk into clearer focus by progressively connecting smaller pieces of the puzzle.

Internal audit typically creates an extensive body of work that can itself be an excellent indicator of directional changes in risk. Auditors tend to be quite granular in their work, but it's possible to step back and consider the separate audits as a series of dots we can connect to create a bigger picture. Accordingly, "connecting the dots" can also be an effective continuous risk monitoring strategy when used in conjunction with a KRI approach.

How to get started: Internal audit leverages the results of completed or ongoing internal audit work to identify systemic issues or trends pointing to emerging or existing risks. For example, they may glean insights on cost or expense overruns due to changing macroeconomic conditions, violations of new regulations, or the unintended consequences of new corporate policies.

Maintenance: Seek feedback from stakeholders and first- and second-line teams on the value of the connected dots approach. Refine as needed.

Monitor External and Internal Indicators of Emerging Risk

For a truly comprehensive view on the ebb and flow of risk, it is imperative to look both beyond—and deeper into—your organization. Methodical reviews of external and internal risk indicators can support monitoring of macroeconomic, political, geopolitical, industry, and other trends.

Emerging risk indicators can be monitored through external resources such as:

- **Third-party research and reports assessing key risks from different perspectives**, such as the WEF's *Global Risks Report* and *Future of Jobs Report*; Protiviti and NC State University's *Executive Perspectives on Top Risks*; the IAF's *Risk in Focus* and *Pulse of Internal Audit* surveys; the Association of Certified Fraud Examiners' (ACFE's) *Report to the Nations* on occupational fraud; and other risk-focused reports from The IIA, Chartered Institute of Internal Auditors (CIIA), the Big Four, and other consulting firms
- **Economic forecasts** generated from myriad sources can be target-rich when identifying emerging risks

- **Media headlines and social media activity** heralding emerging risks
- **Geopolitical and political outlooks** in regions where you're operating, expanding, or investing
- **Legislative and regulatory outlooks** because today's legislative headlines often foretell tomorrow's compliance risks
- **Industry conferences, publications, and trends,** helping you understand the disruptive threats facing your industry and how competitors are responding and performing
- **Customer feedback,** both favorable and unfavorable

Internal resources to monitor include:

- **Strategic business risks as reflected in your organization's strategic plans, goals, and success factors:** focus first on your organization's objectives, which give rise to its risks
- **Planned corporate initiatives (e.g., digital transformation),** which all have risks associated with them
- **Changes to corporate culture,** such as new leaders defining success differently
- **Employee feedback,** both favorable and unfavorable
- **Data, KRIs, and AI analytics** from technologies your company is leveraging

How to get started: Identify internal and external resources to be reviewed on an ongoing basis. Allocate review responsibilities across participating team members to ensure adequate, continuous coverage. Establish protocols and guidelines for sharing key insights.

Maintenance: Monitor the reliability of external and internal emerging risk indicators over time. Refine, add, or remove resources as needed.

Don't Wait Until the Storm Is Overhead

Continuous risk monitoring is an essential element in any connected risk approach. Without it, organizations are likely to find themselves addressing yesterday's challenges—thereby missing many of today's emerging risks and opportunities. Planning, prioritization, and execution must be dynamic in response to changing conditions.

A continuous approach provides significant value to stakeholders, particularly during times of crisis. Indeed, moments of crisis make the need clear. I have often equated emerging risks to being the thunder that precedes the storm. In the world we live in today, we may not be able to wait until we hear the thunder. The speed of light is faster than the speed of sound, so it's the lightning we should be looking for.

Don't wait for the storm to hit your organization. Instead, acknowledge the reality of risk management in permacrisis, and make the shift now. Continuous risk monitoring is a critical way you can futureproof risk management for your organization. It is also one of the building blocks to achieving connected risk maturity—the topic of our next chapter.

CHAPTER 14

The Path to Connected Risk Maturity

Connected risk is a journey; no organization can achieve it all at once. Chances are that there is at least a scintilla of connected risk behavior already taking place within your organization. The important thing is to prioritize risk management transformation and get started. Creating a connected risk vision and strategy for your organization gets you on the path.

If your organization is at square one (or even zero), rest assured you are not alone. Most organizations are in the early stages of implementing connected risk, with varying degrees of informal or formal communication, coordination, and collaboration.

AuditBoard's *2024 Focus on the Future* survey explored the relationship structures and interactions between internal audit and ERM. Recall that many CAEs also have responsibility for ERM, as outlined in chapter 9. In organizations where CAEs do not have this responsibility, however, internal audit and ERM may be missing out on key opportunities. For example:

- Only 9 percent of internal audit leaders report that internal audit and ERM coordinate on all major aspects of managing enterprise risks.
- Another 12 percent jointly identify, assess, and report on enterprise risks but conduct separate risk management effectiveness assessments.
- Half (50 percent) coordinate some work and reporting, but operate independently.
- Lastly, 29 percent report that ERM and internal audit only communicate with each other on an informal basis.[1]

Fortunately, these missed opportunities also represent many of the steps on the path to connected risk maturity. Organizations can begin the journey by improving how they communicate, coordinate, and collaborate on these key aspects of risk management.

If connected risk is a journey, what stages do organizations go through to achieve maturity? There are myriad ways connected risk maturity can be classified. For our current purposes, I choose to delineate maturity on the basis of how people, processes, technology, data, and key stakeholders are engaged in helping an organization manage risks. On that basis, I have identified what I believe are four distinct levels of maturity.

- Stage One: *Communication*
- Stage Two: *Coordination*
- Stage Three: *Collaboration*
- Stage Four: *Connection*

As you read through the descriptions of each stage, ask yourself: Which is closest to your organization's current state? What short-term actions can the organization take to achieve the next stage? What longer-term actions and priorities will support increasing maturity to subsequent stages?

This chapter is intended as a conversation facilitator, supporting productive, positive, and forward-looking discussions about where organizations are on the path to connected risk maturity. It is not intended to devalue any organization's current practices or state of maturity, given the countless excellent reasons organizations may have for being in less mature states. The goal is simply to map a clear path forward that assists each organization in planning and prioritizing its unique connected risk vision.

Start by aligning on a connected risk vision. Then, agree on a plan to attain the vision. In all likelihood, you will identify milestones that align with the connected risk maturity model I outline in this chapter.

Once you have charted a course, it is important to monitor your progress. Advancement may feel slow at times, but incremental progress is nonetheless progress. The only surefire way to fail in reaching any destination is if you never begin the journey in the first place.

Stage One: Communication

The least mature stage on the path to connected risk represents the classical approach to risk management still alive and well in many organizations. While key audit, risk, compliance, and InfoSec players communicate periodically to ensure that other teams are informed about the results of their work, no coordination, collaboration, or genuine connection is taking place. These are the proverbial ships passing in the night, with each team going about their work largely unaware of the other teams' efforts and perspectives.

When assessing the key drivers of connected risk at this stage, the following behaviors are common.

- **People:** Key team members across the three lines do communicate the results of their work in ways that other teams can access or observe. However, there's little happening by way of informal communication or relationship building across the different teams.
- **Processes:** Processes are typically very siloed, such that each team's processes are designed to enable them to meet their very specific purposes (e.g., internal auditors' processes yield engagement results to provide assurance or advice, risk managers' processes generate risk assessments that are provided to management).
- **Technology:** To the extent technology is leveraged, it is designed and implemented to enable the individual teams to achieve their distinct purposes.
- **Data:** Access to data is undertaken by individual teams, often resulting in these teams accessing—and basing their analyses and outputs upon—conflicting or incomplete data sets.
- **Stakeholder support:** Stakeholders are served by each team individually. Results are delivered separately, and stakeholders often express frustration at the lack of alignment between different teams' results and risk taxonomies. Given the lack of coordination, stakeholders are also more likely to discover gaps in coverage of key risks, overlapping efforts on related risks, and duplicative requests for the same information, leading to increased audit fatigue.

Stage Two: Coordination

At stage two, key audit, risk, compliance, and InfoSec team members have realized that a lack of coordination in risk management activities is neither effective nor efficient for their organizations. Accordingly, teams are deliberately undertaking a degree of formal coordination alongside their periodic communications. In other words, their "ships" typically know in advance when the others' ships will be passing, and they sometimes plan their journeys in tandem when conditions are favorable. They are occasionally, but not consistently, sharing maps and insights gleaned from their navigational tools.

When assessing the key drivers of connected risk at this stage, the following behaviors are common.

- **People:** Individual team members recognize the value of more actively coordinating with their counterparts, identifying instances where coordination makes their work easier and results in more timely outputs. Communication is still periodic, but informal communications are now taking place alongside more formal communications.
- **Processes:** While teams still tend to rely on their own processes, they voluntarily coordinate when presented with opportunities to do so (e.g., on timing of risk assessments).
- **Technology:** Control and risk owners may have access to the same technology to respond to risk-related requests (e.g., document requests, control certifications, capturing remediation plans). Beyond this, to the extent technology is leveraged, it is still largely designed and implemented to enable the individual teams to achieve their distinct purposes.
- **Data:** Access is still largely undertaken by individual teams. However, some team members are actively sharing data, particularly when requested by other teams.
- **Stakeholder support:** Stakeholders see value in the increased coordination and improved communication; for example, they appreciate not being repeatedly asked to sit for interviews during the risk assessment process. However, they are still often frustrated by misaligned results, coverage gaps, and inconsistent risk ratings or definitions across teams.

Stage Three: Collaboration

Stage three adds the all-important layer of proactive, ongoing, and strategic collaboration to the foundation of communication and coordination established in earlier stages. In this stage, most audit, risk, compliance, and InfoSec team members recognize and appreciate the value that collaboration brings not only to their own efforts, but also to delivering value to the overall organization. Having graduated well beyond "ships passing in the night," all of the ships are now aligned in a well-coordinated fleet headed to the same destination. Further, members of the different teams regularly visit other teams' ships, passing around maps, consistently sharing the information they glean from their different navigational tools, and planning the next leg of their journey in lock-step.

When assessing the key drivers of connected risk at this stage, the following behaviors are common.

- **People:** Teams across all three lines are working collaboratively together to achieve greater efficiency and effectiveness in achieving both their individual and shared purposes. This means they are regularly sharing resources, coordinating activities, communicating both formally and informally, and building strong relationships.
- **Processes:** Teams conduct joint risk assessments and consolidate reporting whenever possible, and are working toward shared issue tracking. They are unable, however, to drive optimum efficiencies by combining or streamlining core tasks and workflows.
- **Technology:** While teams are working toward sharing controls and data, technology remains disjointed. Technology platforms may have integrations with data source systems that enable a degree of real-time data sharing, but efforts are hampered by the limitations of legacy technologies (e.g., not consistently sharing data, retroactive reporting, function-specific implementations, poor user experience).
- **Data:** Teams readily share access to data and results on an ongoing basis and rely on a unified risk and controls matrix and common risk taxonomy, ensuring that everyone is speaking the same language. However, because there is no unified data core, teams are still often working from different or incomplete data sets.

- **Stakeholder support:** Stakeholders value the increased alignment across teams, clearer risk taxonomy and prioritization, and more comprehensive view on risk, all of which enables them to make more proactive and effective risk-based decisions. Risk management is embedding in many aspects of organizational culture, increasing risk awareness and ownership across the organization. The insights first-line stakeholders receive from their second- and third-line advisors, however, are still more reactive than proactive. First-line teams still seek greater agility, transparency, proactiveness, and risk-based insights.

Stage Four: Connection

Stage four incorporates the purpose-built technology that ties together teams, processes, and data in a truly connected ecosystem. With a unified data core, automation, and AI capabilities supporting crucial tasks and workflows, organizations operating at this stage can drive greater value from the high levels of collaboration established in stage three. Now, everyone is on the same ship at all times, and everyone enjoys uninterrupted access to the same maps, forecasts, and data-based insights gleaned from all the different navigational instruments, which are now in direct communication with one another. Because teams are sharing resources and combining efforts, more journeys tend to reach their destinations successfully—even in stormy seas.

When assessing the key drivers of connected risk at this stage, the following behaviors are common.

- **People:** Teams across the three lines are able to optimize communication, coordination, and collaboration, allowing them to surface and manage more risks and data-driven insights. They bring a collaborative, strategic, results-oriented mindset to their work that fortifies relationships, enhances knowledge sharing, and makes the most of everyone's strengths and potential.
- **Processes:** Intelligent, purpose-built automation and AI-powered enablement (e.g., analytics, control testing, report generation, framework mappings, recommendations) enable teams to

streamline workflows and reduce the burden of repetitive or administrative tasks.

- **Technology:** A fully connected ecosystem ties together all of the content and activities of the organization's audit, risk, compliance, and InfoSec programs (e.g., data, analytics, controls, frameworks, workflows). Every module works together and shares data, and every user has a personalized, automated dashboard that prioritizes and sends reminders regarding needed actions.
- **Data:** A unified data core provides a comprehensive view of risk across the organization and a single source of truth for risks, controls, issues, policies, and more. A single data architecture also enables organizations to leverage continuous monitoring strategies and AI programs more effectively because they can access and analyze the full picture of their data.
- **Stakeholder support:** Connected, aligned teams, processes, and data provide stakeholders across all three lines with data-driven insights, increased agility, faster risk detection and issue resolution, and a truly connected, strategic perspective on risk. This enables them to operate with greater confidence, trust, and assurance. Engagement and ownership increase among first-line stakeholders as they benefit from the consistent, aligned processes and reporting, and risk management is now firmly embedded across the entire organization.

Advancing Connected Risk Maturity

Stage four is eminently worth achieving, but organizations can go further. Connected risk provides the foundations for advancing maturity well beyond what we just outlined. Remember, connected risk is just your "bicycle"—you decide where it takes you. You power it to your destination.

As the evidence we've laid out over the course of this book has shown, the conditions of permacrisis—paired with a stagnating resource pool—are creating a risk exposure gap that demands organizations take action. We must get on a path to driving more value from the risk resources we have. The more we can build upon the promise and potential of connected risk to enhance our organizations' resilience, agility, competitive advantage, and capacity for value protection, realization, and creation, the better equipped we will be to withstand the risk conditions to come. Connected risk simply ensures that we all have a viable path forward.

CHAPTER 15

The Future of Connected Risk Change Agents in the Age of Permacrisis

Connected risk is a dynamic approach to improving collaboration, awareness, and ownership across all three lines, enabling teams to be more effective in seeing and responding to risks. It helps organizations get ahead of risk and better capitalize on its opportunities, even amid constantly changing conditions. In this way, connected risk already aims at "futureproofing" risk management, ensuring that organizations are risk-resilient and agile, able to flex and adapt as the future reveals itself.

Our explorations are not complete, however, without examining what that future may hold, how connected risk is likely to fit into it, and what impact it could have on risk management roles across the three lines.

What might it look like to be a connected risk change agent in the age of permacrisis? What's at stake if we don't heed the call? Most importantly, how will the second half of the 2020s continue to transform who we are, what we do, and how we are valued?

The Persistence of Permacrisis

Permacrisis shows no sign of abating. It will likely persist during the second half of the 2020s, with new developments and crises continuing to transform the macroeconomic, socioeconomic, environmental, technological, geopolitical, political, regulatory, and business landscapes. Technology in particular will bring challenges both unforeseen and unforeseeable, expanding what's possible while precipitating profound changes.

As the Connected Risk Model affirms, organizations face a barrage of external risks while simultaneously striving to overcome daunting internal issues relative to talent, technology, governance, risk management effectiveness, and other aspects of the risk exposure gap. Despite these forces, organizations will persevere in protecting, realizing, and creating value for stakeholders.

Doing business in these conditions is already a daunting prospect, but the second half of the 2020s promises more disruption and transformation. I truly believe we have only seen the proverbial tip of the iceberg. There is much more to come; only time will reveal how much.

We cannot see the massive volume of the iceberg, but it is there. Failing to prepare is a strategic threat not only to our respective audit, risk, compliance, and InfoSec teams, but to the very organizations we serve.

Writing the New Rules

We must equip ourselves to deal with tomorrow's risks. That means coming to terms with the realities of operating in a risk environment in near-constant flux. It means challenging ourselves to think and work in new ways, and redefining our purposes in terms of how we serve our organizations' overall objectives.

The old rules don't apply. The new rules are being written. We can and must play a role in writing them.

When cautioning about the perils of focusing on the wrong risks, I often return to an expression I learned while working for the U.S. Army. For 20 years, I was a civilian working among four-star generals and other military leaders. They would often caution, "We have to be careful that we're not preparing to fight the last war."

This age-old saying originated from an observation made by French military strategist and political leader Charles de Gaulle, who is reported to have said, "Generals are always fighting the last war." The quote reflects the common tendency to assume that the next threat will look like the last one, though it rarely does.

It's human nature to want to gird ourselves—to defend ourselves from the perils we know. When we've been through a difficult or unpleasant experience, those experiences loom large as we assess our fears about the future. We readily see that which we have already learned to recognize. This tendency, however, is both a fallback and a trap.

Our instinct to "fight the last war" is one reason we were so ill-prepared for the great financial crisis of 2007–2008. Organizations, including their internal auditors and risk managers, were focused on fraudulent financial controls because (as chapter 1 showed) that was the enemy we had learned to fear following the fraudulent financial reporting epidemic earlier that decade. So, we hunkered down, single-mindedly designing and testing financial reporting controls, certain our efforts would protect our organizations.

Nobody was really looking at overall risk management effectiveness. That risk caught us unaware, hitting us squarely between the eyes because we assumed the next threat would look like the last one.

This is why all three lines should be locked arm in arm, looking ahead together to see what is coming our way. Certainly, we can't help wanting to look back, surveying the battlefields where we have fought and dissecting the tactics that did and didn't succeed. Hindsight can be helpful. The problem is when it prevents us from regarding the present and future with clear eyes.

To succeed on battlefields we haven't yet seen, foresight is our best weapon. With that goal in mind, what can we see looking five years out?

Five Predictions for the Second Half of the 2020s

1. AI's Ability to Provide Hindsight Will Exceed Our Own

A hidden thread in this book has been a quiet, latent competition between the three lines, as if we all need to watch our backs to avoid losing standing or importance within our organizations. As I hope I've made clear, this attitude is antithetical to our shared objectives. Further, this unproductive line of thinking overlooks the potential "nemesis" that could disintermediate all of us: AI.

In the age of big data, AI's fast-expanding capacity gives it a natural advantage in providing hindsight. For example, from an internal audit perspective, I predict that AI will soon handle the majority of the assurance tasks that have historically been the profession's bread and butter. The internal auditors are not alone, however, in terms of vulnerability. Even today, many risk managers are using AI to shed light on prevailing and emerging industry risks. InfoSec teams are using AI to accelerate their assessment and testing processes by automating data analysis, vulnerability scanning, and other tasks. AI can also streamline reporting processes by automating data collection and generating reports that comply with regulatory requirements.

Overall, I see AI as having incredible potential in its capacity to become a risk management "expert." Accordingly, part of our collective strategy for pursuing connected risk should include leveraging our natural advantages as "human overseers" of risk. If we can't hope to match AI's capacity for hindsight, we will be well-served to elevate our capacities for providing insight and foresight.

AI is likely to challenge the very existence of many professions. This reality, however, reveals another way connected risk provides value: it enables professionals across all three lines to collectively leverage their expertise, knowledge, and insights about the business to create value that AI cannot provide. That said, futureproofing our roles against AI's impact will require a fundamental change in how we think of our core missions.

2. Foresight Will Become Humans' Competitive Advantage

Effective risk management is essentially forward-looking. While hindsight and insight will always be important, foresight is the key capability required.

Foresight is the ability to help your organization anticipate what may happen in the future, seeing around corners and peering a thousand miles ahead. Developing accurate, relevant, high-quality foresight on risk management requires capabilities only humans can offer, including:

- Detailed, nuanced knowledge of the organization that is grounded in direct experience, deep expertise, an understanding of context, and relationships across the organization
- Clear understanding and alignment with the organization's strategy, values, and priorities

- Ethical judgment and decision-making, free from bias or discrimination
- Critical, creative, innovative, intuitive, and genuinely original thinking and problem-solving that are anchored in what's realistic and possible
- Adaptability to changing conditions, strategies, or priorities
- Empathy and emotional intelligence to support effective communication, collaboration, relationship-building, and change management
- The ability to learn new skills and information at will—and more quickly learn from any mistakes

Internal audit, risk management, compliance, and InfoSec teams should focus on leveling up their performance, insight, and precision around risk to provide more effective foresight to their organizations—or be at risk of being disintermediated by AI. To this end, we should be actively using AI in our work (e.g., leveraging advanced predictive analytics to identify potential risks and issues before they materialize) to improve our capacity for insight and foresight.

3. Talent Strategies Will Become a Differentiator

The impact of talent and skills gaps on organizational performance will continue to grow. These gaps are barriers to transformation, relevance, and resilience, such that any organization wishing to remain viable in the next five years must prioritize building out a comprehensive, forward-looking talent management strategy that integrates with the overall strategy.

We won't achieve our transformational priorities without strategically building out our next-generation talent. Just as the next war won't resemble the last one, the next generation of leaders will look different from the current one. Going forward, it will become increasingly important to emphasize strategic acumen, creative and analytical thinking, relationship centricity, an innovative, connected, and collaborative mindset, and diverse expertise, particularly in data science, AI, and technological literacy.

4. Stronger Emphasis on Governance of Culture and AI

As management consultant Peter Drucker famously observed, "culture eats strategy for breakfast." Indeed, the "way things are done around here" often deviates from organizations' professed values. Culture is a timeless and universal risk that can provide a competitive advantage or breathtakingly destroy organizational value. As AI assumes more of our traditional responsibilities, we will be freed up to focus more on culture risks.

I often coach internal auditors who worry that AI will take our place not to worry. I point out what I consider to be the obvious. If we are no longer around, who will provide assurance over the governance of AI itself? The journey toward responsible AI adoption is complex and ongoing. The emerging risks and compliance requirements related to AI will almost certainly warrant a greater focus during the remainder of this decade.

5. Connected Risk Will Be Vital to Value Creation

As I emphasized in chapter 8, a transformational approach to risk management is underway. The traditional three lines approach is giving way to greater communication, coordination, and collaboration—namely, to a connected risk approach to managing organizational risks.

We are literally at the dawn of that era. The coming decade will likely feature greater competition, greater technological innovation, and greater uncertainty. The three lines must join together as collective change agents to play an even larger role in value creation. After all, as we've seen, it is not the risk conditions themselves that ultimately determine whether value is created or destroyed. The deciding factor is how organizations manage these risk conditions.

Navigating Our Possible Futures

I have shared some of my key predictions for the second half of the 2020s. However, I will stop short of predicting the success of the risk, assurance, and information security professions themselves. I cannot make these predictions because there's only so much I can see and control.

I will continue to do my part to help futureproof the value our professions provide. But it's up to you, and countless others like you, to decide where the future takes us. I see three potential scenarios. Which do you choose?

Scenario One: Complacency Causes Us to Nose-Dive

In this version of our future, the strategic risks facing our professions continue to converge, but we fail to answer the call. We make no effort to collaborate or leverage the technology platforms that power connected risk. We also don't prioritize acquiring new skills and prove ineffective in leveraging AI to augment rather than supplant our skills. As a result, AI takes over many of our tasks, and risk management resources in most organizations either flatline or decline. Our organizations are left asking, "Where were my audit, risk, compliance, and InfoSec advisors when I needed them?" The answer: we are no longer an important part of this picture.

Scenario Two: Stay the Course and Glide By

In this slightly more hopeful future, many strategic risks facing our professions do not materialize; accordingly, we take the "safe" route, sufficing with a solely reactive approach. We move from simply communicating with our three lines counterparts to more frequent coordination and even modest collaboration. But we don't leverage connected risk technology or fully embrace its value. We sail neither toward nor away from the storms facing our organizations. We are there when needed, but as advisors we are seen merely as "useful"—not "indispensable."

Scenario Three: Seize the Opportunities and Soar

In this highly possible future, we fully embrace connected risk and proactively enable our organizations by identifying and embracing key risks as pivotal opportunities. We embrace technology and AI as capacity multipliers, and use continuous risk monitoring and assessment to drive dynamic risk insights and planning, effective mitigation, and enhanced value creation. By investing in proactive talent management and cultivating the human skills that make us irreplaceable, we futureproof the value of our professions. In this future, agility, resilience, and connected risk are not understood as methodologies, but rather as mindsets. We are central, utterly indispensable change agents helping create organizations that are risk-resilient in the face of enormous uncertainty.

Change Agents in Uniting Disruption and Transformation

The first half of the 2020s has granted us an invaluable opportunity to learn, adapt, and emerge better prepared for what's next. Whether we endured in our roles or changed course, we have come too far to let the wiles of risk or technology define who we are or the limits of what we can be.

Disruption and transformation will continue to coexist in the next half of the decade. Fortunately, risk management is the key to navigating both, providing the means by which we can harness disruption to drive transformation. We must be the connected risk change agents our organizations need to succeed in the next half of the 2020s.

This is the future I want for risk management. This is the future where we conquer the perilous risk exposure gap—the future that connected risk makes possible. This is the future we are collectively empowered to create.

Notes

Part 1 – The Era of Permacrisis
Chapter 1: Risk Management in the Modern Age

1. Carol Fox, "Understanding the New ISO and COSO Updates," *Risk Management*, June 1, 2018, https://www.rmmagazine.com/articles/article/2018/06/01/-Understanding-the-New-ISO-and-COSO-Updates.
2. Hugh L. Marsh, James C. Treadway, Jr., et al., *Report of the National Commission on Fraudulent Financial Reporting*, October 1987, accessed August 1, 2024, https://docslib.org/doc/8071038/report-of-the-national-commission-on-fraudulent-financial-reporting.
3. Marsh and Treadway et al., *Report of the National Commission*.
4. Kent N. Schneider and Lana Lowe Becker, "Using the COSO model of internal control as a framework for ethics initiatives in business schools," *Journal of Academic and Business Ethics,* January 2011, https://www.aabri.com/manuscripts/10725.pdf, 5.
5. PricewaterhouseCoopers LLP and Committee of Sponsoring Organizations of the Treadway Commission (COSO), "Enterprise Risk Management: Integrated Framework: Executive Summary, Framework, September 2004," *Association Sections, Divisions, Boards, Teams,* September 2004, https://egrove.olemiss.edu/aicpa_assoc/38, n.p.
6. Fox, "Understanding the New ISO and COSO Updates."
7. COSO, "Enterprise Risk Management: Integrating with Strategy and Performance: Executive Summary," June 2017, https://www.coso.org/_files/ugd/3059fc_61ea5985b03c4293960642fdce408eaa.pdf, n.p.
8. Sandrine Tranchard, "ISO celebrates 70 years," ISO, February 23, 2017, https://www.iso.org/news/2017/02/Ref2163.html.
9. International Organization for Standardization (ISO), "Risk Management: ISO 31000," February 2018, https://www.iso.org/files/live/sites/isoorg/files/store/en/PUB100426.pdf, 2.
10. ISO, "Risk Management: ISO 31000," 3.
11. ISO, "Risk Management: ISO 31000," 1.
12. ISO, "Risk Management: ISO 31000," 3.
13. Fox, "Understanding the New ISO and COSO Updates."
14. Peter Bäckman, "Enterprise Risk Management to the 21st Century Resilient Organization," LinkedIn, February 2, 2022, https://www.linkedin.com/pulse/enterprise-risk-management-21st-century-resilient-b%C3%A4ckman-ambci/.

Chapter 2: The Emergence of Permacrisis

1. HarperCollins Publishers, definition of "permacrisis," *Collins English Dictionary*, accessed August 1, 2024, https://www.collinsdictionary.com/us/dictionary/english/permacrisis.
2. Helen Bushby, "Permacrisis declared Collins Dictionary word of the year," BBC, October 31, 2022, https://www.bbc.com/news/entertainment-arts-63458467.
3. Richard F. Chambers, "Risk and Audit Transformation in the Era of Permacrisis: Imperatives for 2024 and Beyond," *AuditBoard* (blog), August 29, 2023, https://www.auditboard.com/blog/risk-and-audit-transformation-in-the-era-of-permacrisis/.
4. Keith Goodwin, "Dodd-Frank Wall Street Reform and Consumer Protection Act of 2010," Federal Reserve History, July 21, 2010, https://www.federalreservehistory.org/essays/dodd-frank-act.
5. John Weinberg, "The Great Recession and Its Aftermath," Federal Reserve History, November 22, 2013, https://www.federalreservehistory.org/essays/great-recession-and-its-aftermath.
6. Howard Schneider and Jonnelle Marte, "From opioid deaths to student debt: A view of the 2010s economy in charts," Reuters, December 31, 2019, https://www.reuters.com/article/world/from-opioid-deaths-to-student-debt-a-view-of-the-2010s-economy-in-charts-idUSKBN1YZ0AD/.
7. Richard F. Chambers, "Ready or Not — Here Come the 2020s," *Audit Beacon* (blog), October 7, 2019, https://www.richardchambers.com/ready-or-not-here-come-the-2020s/.
8. Richard F. Chambers, "The Road Ahead for Internal Audit: 5 Bold Predictions for the 2020s," *Audit Beacon* (blog), November 4, 2019, https://www.richardchambers.com/the-road-ahead-for-internal-audit-5-bold-predictions-for-the-2020s/.
9. Frederick Kempe, "Here are six reasons to be optimistic about 2020," CNBC, December 21, 2019, https://www.cnbc.com/2019/12/20/here-are-six-reasons-to-be-optimistic-about-2020.html.
10. "Coronavirus: the first three months as it happened," *Nature*, April 22, 2020, https://doi.org/10.1038/d41586-020-00154-w.
11. Alasdair Sandford, "Coronavirus: Half of humanity now on lockdown as 90 countries call for confinement," *EuroNews*, February 4, 2020, https://www.euronews.com/2020/04/02/coronavirus-in-europe-spain-s-death-toll-hits-10-000-after-record-950-new-deaths-in-24-hou.
12. Lawrence H. Leith, "What caused the high inflation during the COVID-19 period?," *Monthly Labor Review*, U.S. Bureau of Labor Statistics, December 2023, https://www.bls.gov/opub/mlr/2023/beyond-bls/what-caused-the-high-inflation-during-the-covid-19-period.htm.
13. Irina Ivanova, "Inflation hit 9.1% in June, highest rate in more than 40 years," MoneyWatch, CBS News, July 13, 2022, https://www.cbsnews.com/news/inflation-june-cpi-report-hit-new-high-40-years-9-1-percent/.

14. Drew DeSilver, "Most U.S. bank failures have come in a few big waves," Pew Research Center, April 11, 2023, https://www.pewresearch.org/short-reads/2023/04/11/most-u-s-bank-failures-have-come-in-a-few-big-waves/.

Chapter 3: The Speed of Risk and Value Destruction

1. Ingrid Lexova and Umer Khan, "US bankruptcies hit 13-year peak in 2023; 50 new filings in December," S&P Global, January 9, 2024, https://www.spglobal.com/marketintelligence/en/news-insights/latest-news-headlines/us-bankruptcies-hit-13-year-peak-in-2023-50-new-filings-in-december-79967180.
2. Ian Bezek, "7 Companies That Went Bankrupt Due to COVID," *U.S. News & World Report*, May 12, 2023, https://money.usnews.com/investing/stock-market-news/slideshows/covid-bankrupt-companies.
3. Khristopher J. Brooks, "3 key mistakes that doomed Bed Bath & Beyond," MoneyWatch, CBS News, January 13, 2023, https://www.cbsnews.com/news/bed-bath-beyond-retail-collapse-stores/.
4. "The Death of a Giant: Bed Bath & Beyond's Downward Spiral to Irrelevance," From, accessed August 7, 2024, https://www.from.digital/insights/death-giant-bed-bath-beyonds-downward-spiral-irrelevance/.
5. "Number of Bed Bath & Beyond stores worldwide from 2015 to 2022," Statista, December 1, 2023, https://www.statista.com/statistics/1076094/store-numbers-of-bed-bath-and-beyond-worldwide/.
6. Brooks, "3 key mistakes."
7. Angie Basiouny, "What Went Wrong at Bed Bath & Beyond," Knowledge at Wharton, May 2, 2023, https://knowledge.wharton.upenn.edu/article/what-went-wrong-at-bed-bath-beyond/.
8. Jordyn Holman, "Overstock.com Wins $21.5 Million Bid for Bed Bath & Beyond's Assets," *The New York Times*, June 22, 2023, https://www.nytimes.com/2023/06/22/business/bed-bath-beyond-overstock-bankruptcy.html.
9. Reuters, "Why did WeWork fail, and what is next for the company?," November 8, 2023, https://www.reuters.com/business/why-wework-failed-what-is-next-2023-11-07/.
10. Reuters, "Why did WeWork fail."
11. Ross Garlick, "A Recap of WeWork's almighty implosion," Ross Rambles, June 11, 2020, https://rossgarlick.com/2020/06/11/a-recap-of-weworks-almighty-implosion/.
12. WSJ Real Estate, "WeWork: A $20 Billion Startup Fueled by Silicon Valley Pixie Dust," *The Wall Street Journal*, October 19, 2017, https://www.wsj.com/articles/wework-a-20-billion-startup-fueled-by-silicon-valley-pixie-dust-1508435003.
13. NPR, "WeWork has filed for bankruptcy. Here's a look at its downfall," November 7, 2023, https://www.npr.org/2023/11/07/1211333582/wework-has-filed-for-bankruptcy-heres-a-look-at-its-downfall.
14. Reuters, "Why did WeWork fail."

15. Matt Turner, "A bunch of cycling enthusiasts just helped Peloton Cycle raise $325 million — betting it could be 'the Apple of fitness'," *Business Insider*, May 24, 2017, https://www.businessinsider.com/peloton-raises-325-million-2017-5.

16. Tom Huddleston, Jr., "How Peloton exercise bikes became a $4 billion fitness start-up with a cult following," CNBC Make It, February 12, 2019, https://www.cnbc.com/2019/02/12/how-peloton-exercise-bikes-and-streaming-gained-a-cult-following.html.

17. Gabrielle Fonrouge, "Inside Peloton's rapid rise and bitter fall — and its attempt at a comeback," CNBC, February 19, 2023, https://www.cnbc.com/2023/02/19/peloton-rise-fall-attempted-comeback.html.

18. Fonrouge, "Inside Peloton's rapid rise."

19. Fonrouge, "Inside Peloton's rapid rise."

20. Tom Wilson, "Crypto exchange FTX valued at $32 bln as SoftBank invests," Reuters, January 31, 2022, https://www.reuters.com/markets/us/crypto-exchange-ftx-valued-32-bln-softbank-invests-2022-01-31/.

21. Angus Berwick, "Exclusive: At least $1 billion of client funds missing at failed crypto firm FTX," Reuters, November 13, 2022, https://www.reuters.com/markets/currencies/exclusive-least-1-billion-client-funds-missing-failed-crypto-firm-ftx-sources-2022-11-12/.

22. David Yaffe-Bellany, "New Chief Calls FTX's Corporate Control a 'Complete Failure'," *The New York Times*, November 17, 2022, https://www.nytimes.com/2022/11/17/business/ftx-bankruptcy.html.

23. Richard F. Chambers and Anthony Pugliese, "On the Frontlines: The Hard Lessons of FTX," *AuditBoard* (blog), January 25, 2023, https://www.auditboard.com/blog/on-the-frontlines-the-hard-lessons-of-ftx/.

24. Luc Cohen and Jody Godoy, "Bankman-Fried sentenced to 25 years for multi-billion dollar FTX fraud," Reuters, March 28, 2024, https://www.reuters.com/technology/sam-bankman-fried-be-sentenced-multi-billion-dollar-ftx-fraud-2024-03-28/.

25. "About Zoom," *Zoom* (blog), accessed August 6, 2024, https://www.zoom.com/en/about/.

26. Dominic Kent, "The History Of Eric Yuan's Zoom," Mio, accessed August 6, 2024, https://www.m.io/blog/eric-yuan-zoom.

27. Steven Loeb, "When Zoom was young: the early years," Vator News, March 26, 2020, https://vator.tv/news/2020-03-26-when-zoom-was-young-the-early-years.

28. Loeb, "When Zoom was young."

29. Robbie Pleasant, "Zoom Video Communications Reaches 1 Million Participants," TMCnet, 2013, https://www.tmcnet.com/topics/articles/2013/05/23/339279-zoom-video-communications-reaches-1-million-participants.htm.

30. Kent, "The History Of Eric Yuan's Zoom."

31. Jon Quast, "Can Zoom Make You . . .Happy?," The Motley Fool, October 24, 2019, https://www.fool.com/investing/2019/10/24/can-zoom-make-youhappy.aspx.
32. "A Message from Eric Yuan, CEO of Zoom," *Zoom* (blog), February 7, 2023, https://www.zoom.com/en/blog/a-message-from-eric-yuan-ceo-of-zoom/.
33. Yitzi Weiner, "The Inspiring Backstory of Eric S. Yuan, Founder and CEO of Zoom," Thrive Global, October 2, 2017, Internet Archive Wayback Machine, accessed August 6, 2024, https://web.archive.org/web/20190423220431/https://medium.com/thrive-global/the-inspiring-backstory-of-eric-s-yuan-founder-and-ceo-of-zoom-98b7fab8cacc.
34. Brian Caulfield, "NVIDIA Founder and CEO Jensen Huang Returns to Denny's Where NVIDIA Launched a Trillion-Dollar Vision," Nvidia, September 26, 2023, https://blogs.nvidia.com/blog/nvidia-dennys-trillion/.
35. Rob Wile, "Why everyone is suddenly talking about Nvidia, the nearly $3 trillion-dollar company fueling the AI revolution," NBC News, February 24, 2024, https://www.nbcnews.com/business/business-news/what-is-nvidia-what-do-they-make-ai-artificial-intelligence-rcna140171.
36. Andrew Nusca, "This Man Is Leading an AI Revolution in Silicon Valley—And He's Just Getting Started," *Fortune*, December 1, 2017, Internet Archive Wayback Machine, accessed August 6, 2024, https://web.archive.org/web/20171116192021/http://fortune.com/2017/11/16/nvidia-ceo-jensen-huang/.
37. "Our Story," Nvidia, 2024, accessed August 1, 2024, https://images.nvidia.com/pdf/NVIDIA-Story.pdf.
38. Peter Sayer, "How Nvidia became a trillion-dollar company," *CIO*, September 1, 2023, https://www.cio.com/article/646471/how-nvidia-became-a-trillion-dollar-company.html.
39. Tom Huddleston, Jr., "Nvidia CEO built a $3 trillion company with this leadership philosophy: 'No task is beneath me'," CNBC Make It, July 6, 2024, https://www.cnbc.com/2024/07/06/nvidia-ceos-leadership-philosophy-no-task-is-beneath-me.html.
40. Maddie Berg, "CS undergrad wins tech fellowship," *The Brown Daily Herald,* September 9, 2012, https://www.browndailyherald.com/article/2012/09/cs-undergrad-wins-tech-fellowship.
41. Josh Constine, "23-Year-Old's Design Collaboration Tool Figma Launches With $14M To Fight Adobe," *TechCrunch*, December 3, 2015, https://techcrunch.com/2015/12/03/figma-vs-goliath/.
42. Dylan Field, "Reflecting on Figma's First Year," Figma Shortcut, May 20, 2017, https://www.figma.com/blog/reflecting-on-figmas-first-year/.
43. Dylan Field, "Meet us in the browser," Figma Shortcut, December 9, 2020, https://www.figma.com/blog/meet-us-in-the-browser/.
44. Monica Chin, "Education Chromebooks are getting Figma, a very cool set of design tools," The Verge, June 7, 2022, https://www.theverge.com/2022/6/7/23157093/google-chromebook-students-figma-figjam-partnership.

45. David Wadhwani, "We're thrilled to announce Adobe's intent to acquire Figma," Adobe, accessed August 6, 2024, https://www.adobe.com/about-adobe/intent-to-acquire-20220915.html.
46. John Naughton, "Adobe can't Photoshop out the fact its $20bn Figma deal is a naked land grab," *The Guardian*, September 24, 2022, https://www.theguardian.com/commentisfree/2022/sep/24/adobe-cant-photoshop-out-the-fact-its-20bn-figma-deal-is-a-naked-land-grab.
47. Michael J. de la Merced, "Adobe Scraps Its $20 Billion Takeover of Figma," *The New York Times*, December 18, 2023, https://www.nytimes.com/2023/12/18/business/adobe-figma-takeover.html.
48. Caleb Naysmith, "Adobe Failed To Acquire Figma; Now Figma is a Bigger Threat Than Ever After A $1 Billion Payday And New Acquisition On The Horizon," Yahoo! Finance, March 5, 2024, https://finance.yahoo.com/news/adobe-failed-acquire-figma-now-153236860.html.
49. Field, "Meet us in the browser."

Part 2 – The Widening Risk Exposure Gap
Chapter 4: The Daunting Risk Landscape

1. IBM and the Ponemon Institute, *Cost of a Data Breach Report 2024*, accessed August 7, 2024, https://www.ibm.com/reports/data-breach.
2. Protiviti and NC State Poole College of Management Enterprise Risk Management Initiative, *Executive Perspectives on Top Risks for 2024 and a Decade Later*, 2024, https://www.protiviti.com/sites/default/files/2024-03/nc-state-protiviti-survey-top-risks_2024-2034.pdf, 12.
3. Protiviti and The Institute of Internal Auditors (IIA), *Navigating a Technology Risk-Filled Horizon: Assessing the results of the Global Technology Audit Risks Survey conducted by Protiviti and the Institute of Internal Auditors*, 2023, https://www.protiviti.com/sites/default/files/2023-10/protiviti-11th-annual-global-technology-audit-risks-survey-iia-global.pdf, 3.
4. Protiviti and The IIA, *Navigating a Technology Risk-Filled Horizon*, 12.
5. KPMG, *2023 Chief Risk Officer Survey: Navigating compounding threats and emerging opportunities in a fast-moving world*, 2023, https://kpmg.com/kpmg-us/content/dam/kpmg/pdf/2023/cro-survey.pdf, 5.
6. Cyentia Institute and SecurityScorecard, "Cyentia Institute and SecurityScorecard Research Report: Close Encounters of the Third (and Fourth) Party Kind," SecurityScorecard, February 1, 2023, https://securityscorecard.com/research/cyentia-close-encounters-of-the-third-and-fourth-party-kind/.
7. Protiviti and NC State, *Executive Perspectives*, 3.
8. World Economic Forum (WEF), Marsh McLennan, and Zurich Insurance Group, *The Global Risks Report 2024*, January 2024, https://www3.weforum.org/docs/WEF_The_Global_Risks_Report_2024.pdf, 8.

9. ISACA, "Generative AI: The Risks, Opportunities and Outlook," 2023, https://www.isaca.org/-/media/files/isacadp/project/isaca/resources/infographics/generative-ai-2023-global-infographic-1025.pdf, n.p.
10. WEF, *The Global Risks Report 2024,* 8.
11. Protiviti and NC State, *Executive Perspectives,* 9.
12. Protiviti and NC State, *Executive Perspectives,* 3.
13. "Data Protection and Privacy Legislation Worldwide," UN Trade & Development (UNCTAD), accessed August 5, 2024, https://unctad.org/page/data-protection-and-privacy-legislation-worldwide.
14. "US State Privacy Legislation Tracker," International Association of Privacy Professionals (IAPP), accessed August 5, 2024, https://iapp.org/resources/article/us-state-privacy-legislation-tracker/.
15. Adam Satariano, "Meta Fined $1.3 Billion for Violating E.U. Data Privacy Rules," *The New York Times*, May 22, 2023, https://www.nytimes.com/2023/05/22/business/meta-facebook-eu-privacy-fine.html.
16. Adam Pajakowski and Kristen Rohrer, *Privacy and Data Protection—Part 3: Insights into Effective Collaboration Between Internal Auditors and Data Privacy Professionals*, Crowe and the Internal Audit Foundation (IAF), February 2024, https://www.theiia.org/globalassets/site/content/research/foundation/2024/crowe-iaf-privacy-and-data-protection-report-part3.pdf, 11.
17. Protiviti and NC State, *Executive Perspectives,* 3.
18. Protiviti and NC State, *Executive Perspectives,* 10.
19. Protiviti and NC State, *Executive Perspectives,* 3.
20. WEF, *The Global Risks Report 2024,* 8.
21. KPMG, *2023 Chief Risk Officer Survey,* 5.
22. IAF, *2024 Risk in Focus: Hot Topics for Internal Auditors—North America*, 2023, https://www.theiia.org/en/internal-audit-foundation/latest-research-and-products/risk-in-focus/, 9.
23. "What Is Globalization?", Peterson Institute for International Economics, last updated October 24, 2022, accessed on August 5, 2024, https://www.piie.com/microsites/globalization/what-is-globalization.
24. WEF, *The Global Risks Report 2024,* 4.
25. Ernst & Young LLP (EY), *Global Board Risk Survey 2023*, 2023, https://www.ey.com/content/dam/ey-unified-site/ey-com/en-gl/campaigns/global-board-risk-survey/documents/ey-global-board-risk-survey-2023.pdf, 9.
26. Protiviti and NC State, *Executive Perspectives,* 3.
27. Protiviti and NC State, *Executive Perspectives,* 3, 5.
28. KPMG, *2023 Chief Risk Officer Survey,* 5.
29. IAF, *2024 Risk in Focus—North America,* 15.
30. KPMG, *Stepping up to a new level of compliance: KPMG Global Chief Ethics and Compliance Officer Survey*, 2024, https://assets.kpmg.com/content/dam/kpmg/xx/pdf/2024/01/stepping-up-to-a-new-level-of-compliance.pdf, 4.

31. Protiviti and NC State, *Executive Perspectives,* 3.
32. EY, *Global Board Risk Survey 2023,* 9.
33. Protiviti and NC State, *Executive Perspectives,* 5.
34. EY, *Global Board Risk Survey 2023,* 9.
35. EY, "The 2022 EY US Generation Survey: Addressing diverse workplace preferences," 2022, accessed August 7, 2024, https://www.ey.com/en_us/diversity-equity-inclusiveness/the-2022-ey-us-generation-survey.
36. "Organizational Culture," Gallup, accessed August 5, 2024, https://www.gallup.com/471521/indicator-organizational-culture.aspx.

Chapter 5: Stagnant Resources

1. Protiviti and NC State, *Executive Perspectives,* 3.
2. Protiviti and NC State, *Executive Perspectives,* 5.
3. McKinsey Digital, *Technology Trends Outlook 2023*, July 2023, https://www.mckinsey.com/~/media/mckinsey/business%20functions/mckinsey%20digital/our%20insights/the%20top%20trends%20in%20tech%202023/mckinsey-technology-trends-outlook-2023-v5.pdf, 5.
4. Protiviti and The IIA, *Navigating a Technology Risk-Filled Horizon,* 31–32.
5. ISC2, *ISC2 Cybersecurity Workforce Study: How the Economy, Skills Gap and Artificial Intelligence are Challenging the Global Cybersecurity Workforce*, 2023, https://media.isc2.org/-/media/Project/ISC2/Main/Media/documents/research/ISC2_Cybersecurity_Workforce_Study_2023.pdf, 5–6.
6. Deloitte and the Center for Audit Quality (CAQ), *Audit Committee Practices Report: Common Threads Across Audit Committees*, 2024, https://www2.deloitte.com/content/dam/Deloitte/us/Documents/audit/us-caq-deloitte-audit-committee-practices-report_2024-03-v2.pdf, 5.
7. Trevor Treharne, "Plugging the risk management talent gap," *Strategic Risk*, October 18, 2023, https://www.strategic-risk-global.com/risk-leaders/plugging-the-risk-management-talent-gap/1445897.article.
8. Susan M. Collins and Robert P. Casey, Jr., *America's Aging Workforce: Opportunities and Challenges*, United States Senate Special Committee on Aging, December 2017, https://www.aging.senate.gov/imo/media/doc/Aging%20Workforce%20Report%20FINAL.pdf, 3–4.
9. Association of International Certified Professional Accountants (AICPA), *2023 Trends Report*, 2023, https://www.thiswaytocpa.com/collectedmedia/files/trends-report-2023.pdf, 5.
10. Mark Maurer, "Accounting Graduates Drop By Highest Percentage in Years," *The Wall Street Journal*, October 12, 2023, https://www.wsj.com/articles/accounting-graduates-drop-by-highest-percentage-in-years-5720cd0f.
11. Mark Maurer, "Job Security Isn't Enough to Keep Many Accountants From Quitting," *The Wall Street Journal*, September 22, 2023, https://www.wsj.com/articles/accounting-quit-job-security-675fc28f?.

12. The Risk Management Society (RIMS), *RIMS Risk Management Talent 2025 Report*, 2019, https://webapps.rims.org/RiskWorld2023DigPub/static/publications/pdfDownload/RIMS-Risk-Management-Talent-2025-Report.pdf, 1.
13. Protiviti, *2023 Next-Generation Internal Audit Survey*, 2023, https://www.protiviti.com/gl-en/survey/next-gen-ia-2023.
14. WEF, *Future of Jobs Report 2023*, May 2023, https://www3.weforum.org/docs/WEF_Future_of_Jobs_2023.pdf, 5–6.
15. ISACA, "Generative AI," n.p.
16. Joe Edwards, "The Jobs Most at Risk From AI," *Newsweek*, accessed on August 6, 2024, https://www.msn.com/en-us/news/other/the-jobs-most-at-risk-from-ai/ar-BB1oylz8?ocid=BingNewsVerp.
17. Accenture, *A new era of generative AI for everyone*, 2023, https://www.accenture.com/content/dam/accenture/final/accenture-com/document/Accenture-A-New-Era-of-Generative-AI-for-Everyone.pdf, 11.
18. edX For Business, *The 2023 edX AI Survey: Navigating the Workplace in the Age of AI,* 2023, https://business.edx.org/white-paper/navigating-the-workplace-in-the-age-of-ai, 4.
19. David Streitfeld, "If A.I. Can Do Your Job, Maybe It Can Also Replace Your C.E.O.," *The New York Times*, May 28, 2024, https://www.nytimes.com/2024/05/28/technology/ai-chief-executives.html.
20. WEF, *Future of Jobs Report 2023,* 7.
21. University of Phoenix, *The University of Phoenix Career Optimism Index 2024*, March 2024, https://www.phoenix.edu/content/dam/edu/career-institute/doc/uopx-career-optimism-index-2024-research-findings-dma-snapshots.pdf, 8.

Chapter 6: The Unsustainable Risk Exposure Gap

1. Protiviti and NC State, *Executive Perspectives,* 3.
2. Richard F. Chambers, *2024 Focus on the Future Report*, AuditBoard, November 16, 2023, https://www.auditboard.com/resources/ebook/2024-focus-on-the-future-report-widening-risk-exposure-gap-demands-internal-audit-transformation/, 22.
3. Liam Tung, "Log4j flaw: Why it will still be causing problems a decade from now," ZDNET, July 15, 2022, https://www.zdnet.com/article/log4j-flaw-why-it-will-still-be-causing-problems-a-decade-from-now/.
4. Consortium for Information & Software Quality (CISQ), *Cost of Poor Software Quality in the U.S.: A 2022 Report*, accessed August 6, 2024, https://www.it-cisq.org/the-cost-of-poor-quality-software-in-the-us-a-2022-report/#.
5. PwC, *The Resilience Revolution is Here: PwC's Global Crisis and Resilience Survey 2023*, 2023, https://www.pwc.com/gx/en/crisis/pwc-global-crisis-resilience-survey-2023.pdf, 2.
6. Peter Bäckman, "Enterprise Risk Management."

7. WEF and McKinsey & Company, *Building a Resilient Tomorrow: Concrete Actions for Global Leaders*, January 2024, https://www.mckinsey.com/~/media/mckinsey/business%20functions/risk/our%20insights/building%20a%20resilient%20tomorrow%20concrete%20actions%20for%20global%20leaders/wef_building_a_resilient_tomorrow_2024.pdf, 4.
8. WEF, *Future of Jobs Report 2023*, 6.

Part 3 – Siloed Risk Management Creates Its Own Risks
Chapter 7: Risk Management Is the Means, Not the End

1. COSO, "ERM: Executive Summary," 3.
2. The IIA, *Global Internal Audit Standards*, January 9, 2024, https://www.theiia.org/globalassets/site/standards/editable-versions/globalinternalauditstandards_2024january9_editable.pdf, 15.
3. The IIA, "Standard 7.1 Organizational Independence," *Standards*, 46.
4. Richard F. Chambers with Robert Perez, *Agents of Change: Internal Auditors in the Era of Permacrisis, Second Edition* (Location: Fina Press, 2024), 33.
5. The IIA, *The IIA's Three Lines Model: An update of the Three Lines of Defense*, July 2020, https://www.theiia.org/globalassets/documents/resources/the-iias-three-lines-model-an-update-of-the-three-lines-of-defense-july-2020/three-lines-model-updated-english.pdf, 7.
6. The IIA, "Principle 5: Third line independence," *The IIA's Three Lines Model* (2020), 3.
7. The IIA, "Standard 7.1 Organizational Independence," *Standards*, 45–47.
8. The IIA, "Standard 9.5 Coordination and Reliance," *Standards*, 69.
9. The IIA, "Standard 9.5 Coordination and Reliance," *Standards*, 70.
10. The IIA, "Standard 9.3 Methodologies," *Standards*, 65.
11. The IIA, "Standard 11.1 Building Relationships and Communicating with Stakeholders," *Standards*, 77.
12. The IIA, "Standard 10.3 Technological Resources," *Standards*, 76.
13. The IIA, "Standard 3.1 Competency," *Standards*, 26.
14. Peter Bäckman, "Enterprise Risk Management."

Chapter 8: Beyond the Three Lines Approach

1. Federation of European Risk Management Associations (FERMA) and the European Confederation of Institutes of Internal Auditing (ECIIA), *Guidance on the 8th EU Company Law Directive*, September 21, 2010, https://www.ferma.eu/app/uploads/2011/09/eciia-ferma-guidance-on-the-8th-eu-company-law-directive.pdf, 6.
2. FERMA and ECIAA, *Guidance*, 9.
3. The IIA, *The Three Lines of Defense in Effective Risk Management and Control*, January 2013, https://theiia.fi/wp-content/uploads/2017/01/pp-the-three-lines-of-defense-in-effective-risk-management-and-control.pdf, 1–2.

4. The IIA, *Three Lines of Defense* (2013), 5.
5. The IIA, *Three Lines of Defense* (2013), 4.
6. "IIA Issues Important Update to Three Lines Model," The IIA, July 20, 2020, https://www.theiia.org/en/content/communications/2020/july/20-july-2020-iia-issues-important-update-to-three-lines-model/.
7. The IIA, *Three Lines Model* (2020), 3–4.
8. The IIA, *Three Lines of Defense* (2013), 7.
9. The IIA, "IIA Issues Important Update."
10. The IIA, *Three Lines Model* (2020), 3.
11. COSO, "ERM: Executive Summary," 3.

Part 4 – The Connected Risk Imperative
Chapter 9: Fostering Connected Risk Thinking

1. COSO, "ERM: Executive Summary," 1.
2. COSO, "ERM: Executive Summary," 1.
3. IAF, *2024 North American Pulse of Internal Audit: Benchmarks for Internal Audit Leaders*, March 2024, https://www.theiia.org/en/resources/research-and-reports/pulse/, 5–6.
4. The IIA, "Standard 9.5 Coordination and Reliance," *Standards*, 70.

Chapter 10: Attributes of Connected Risk Thinkers

1. Richard F. Chambers, *Trusted Advisors: Key Attributes of Outstanding Internal Auditors* (Flagler Beach, FL: Fina Press, 2024), 69.
2. The IIA, "Standard 9.5 Coordination and Reliance," *Standards*, 69.

Chapter 11: Technology—from Impediment to Enabler

1. Gartner, "Integrated Risk Management (IRM) Solutions Reviews and Ratings," accessed August 6, 2024, https://www.gartner.com/reviews/market/integrated-risk-management.

Chapter 12: The "Wow Factor" from Connected Risk Alignment

1. Richard F. Chambers, "Navigating 2023's Risk Riptides Requires All Hands On Deck," *Forbes*, February 28, 2023, https://www.forbes.com/sites/forbesbusinesscouncil/2023/02/28/navigating-2023s-risk-riptides-requires-all-hands-on-deck/.

Part 5 – Futureproofing for Risk Resilience
Chapter 13: Continuous Risk Monitoring

1. COSO, "ERM: Executive Summary," 6.
2. 2. The IIA, "Standard 9.4 Internal Audit Plan," *Standards*, 67.

3. 3. U.S. Department of Commerce National Institute of Standards and Technology (NIST), *NIST Special Publication 800-137: Information Security Continuous Monitoring (ISCM) for Federal Information Systems and Organizations*, September 2011, https://nvlpubs.nist.gov/nistpubs/legacy/sp/nistspecialpublication800-137.pdf, vi.
4. NIST, *NIST SP 800-137*, vi.
5. U.S. Securities and Exchange Commission (SEC), *17 CFR Parts 229, 232, 239, 240, and 249, RIN 3235-AM89, Cybersecurity Risk Management, Strategy, Governance, and Incident Disclosure* (Final Rule), 2023, https://www.sec.gov/files/rules/final/2023/33-11216.pdf, n.p.
6. U.S. SEC, *17 CFR 210, 229, 230, 232, 239, and 249, RIN 3235-AM87, The Enhancement and Standardization of Climate-Related Disclosures for Investors* (Final Rule), 2024, https://www.sec.gov/files/rules/final/2024/33-11275.pdf, n.p.
7. Protiviti, *2023 Next-Generation Internal Audit Survey.*
8. IAF, *2024 Risk in Focus—North America*, 32.
9. J.P. Thompson, R.P. Mahajan, "Monitoring the monitors—beyond risk management," *British Journal of Anaesthesia*, Volume 97, Issue 1, 2006, https://doi.org/10.1093/bja/ael139, 1–3.
10. NIST, *NIST SP 800-137*, vii.
11. NIST, *NIST SP 800-137*, vi.
12. Richard F. Chambers, *2023 Focus on the Future Report*, AuditBoard, December 1, 2022, https://www.auditboard.com/resources/ebook/2023-focus-on-the-future-internal-audit-must-accelerate-its-response-in-addressing-key-risks/, 14.
13. Mark S. Beasley, Bruce C. Branson, and Bonnie V. Hancock, *Developing Key Risk Indicators to Strengthen Enterprise Risk Management*, COSO, 2010, iii.

Chapter 14: The Path to Connected Risk Maturity

1. Chambers, *2024 Focus on the Future*, 22.